Contents

1 Chapter 1: Introduction to Data Warehousing

A data warehouse is a subject-oriented, integrated, time-variant, and non-volatile collection of data designed to support management's decision-making process. It's a central repository where data from multiple sources is consolidated, cleaned, and transformed into a structured format suitable for analysis. Unlike operational databases, which are optimized for transactional processing, data warehouses are optimized for complex queries and analysis. Think of it as a library carefully organized with historical information, ready to be consulted for insights. This distinct separation allows businesses to analyze past trends and performance without impacting the performance of their day-to-day operations. The focus is on providing a comprehensive view of the business, enabling informed decision-making. This consolidated view is crucial for understanding overall performance and identifying areas for improvement.

Several core concepts are essential for understanding the data warehousing landscape. A data mart is a subset of a data warehouse focused on a specific business area, like sales or marketing. It provides a more targeted view of the data, making it easier for specific departments to access and analyze relevant information. Online Analytical Processing (OLAP) is a technology that enables multidimensional analysis of data, allowing users to drill down, roll up, and slice and dice data to explore different perspectives. Extract, Transform, Load (ETL) is the process of extracting data from various sources, transforming it into a consistent format, and loading it into the data warehouse. This process ensures data quality and consistency within the warehouse.

The evolution of data warehousing has been driven by the growing need for businesses to leverage their data for strategic advantage. In the early days, businesses relied on operational systems for reporting, which often proved inefficient and inadequate for complex analysis. The need for a dedicated system for analytical processing became clear. Decision support systems emerged as an early form of data warehousing, but they were limited in scope and scalability. The emergence of relational database technology paved the way for the development of enterprise data warehouses, capable of handling massive volumes of data from diverse sources. The shift from operational to analytical processing marked a significant advancement in business intelligence. This evolution continues with the adoption of cloud-based warehousing and the integration of data lakes, enabling greater agility and scalability.

The primary purpose of a data warehouse is to provide a single source of truth for business intelligence and reporting. By consolidating data from various operational systems and external sources, it eliminates data silos and inconsistencies. This unified view allows for a more accurate and comprehensive understanding of business performance. It enables analysts to perform trend analysis, identify patterns, and make data-driven predictions. Data warehousing empowers organizations to gain a deeper understanding of customer behavior, market trends, and operational efficiencies. This, in turn, leads to better decision-making, improved strategic planning, and ultimately, increased profitability. Imagine a retail company wanting to understand customer purchasing patterns across different regions and time periods. A data warehouse can provide the necessary data to answer these questions, enabling the company to tailor marketing campaigns, optimize inventory management, and improve overall sales performance. Data warehousing plays a critical role in the broader context of business intelligence and data analytics. It serves as the foundation for building analytical applications, dashboards, and reports. By providing clean, consistent, and historical data, the data warehouse enables organizations to extract meaningful insights and make informed decisions. This is a far cry from simply collecting data; it's about transforming data into actionable knowledge. This knowledge can be used to improve operational efficiency, identify new business opportunities, and gain a competitive edge in the market. The ability to analyze historical data is critical for understanding past performance and predicting future trends. This predictive capability allows businesses to anticipate market changes and proactively adjust their strategies. Data warehousing is not merely a technical solution; it's a strategic asset that empowers organizations to unlock the full potential of their data. It's an investment in informed decision-making and long-term business success.

1.1 The Data Warehouse Defined

A data warehouse is a subject-oriented, integrated, time-variant, and non-volatile collection of data designed to support management's decision-making process. Let's break down each component of this definition. Subject-oriented means the data warehouse is organized around key subjects of the business, like customers, products, or sales, rather than operational processes. This allows for easier analysis and reporting on specific business areas. Integration is crucial because data is typically drawn from multiple disparate sources. These sources might include transactional systems, CRM applications, marketing databases, and external data feeds. The data warehouse integrates this data into a consistent format, resolving inconsistencies and redundancies. This unified view is essential for obtaining a holistic understanding of the business. The time-variant nature of a data warehouse means data is tracked over time. This historical context allows for trend analysis, performance comparisons, and forecasting. Data in a data warehouse is typically stored with timestamps or time periods, enabling users to analyze how metrics have changed. Finally, non-volatile signifies that data in the data warehouse is not updated in real-time like operational systems. Instead, data is loaded into the warehouse periodically, typically in batches. This ensures data consistency and allows for efficient querying and analysis without impacting the performance of operational systems. Once loaded, the data remains static for reporting and analysis purposes.

Imagine a retail company with various data sources: point-of-sale systems, online order databases, customer relationship management software, and marketing campaign data. A data warehouse pulls information from all these disparate sources, cleanses it, transforms it into a consistent format, and stores it historically. This allows analysts to track sales trends over time, analyze customer behavior across different channels, and evaluate the effectiveness of marketing campaigns. They can answer questions like: How did sales perform this quarter compared to the same quarter last year? Which product categories are growing the fastest? What are the demographics of our most profitable customers? These insights are not readily available from individual operational systems due to data silos and differing formats.

The benefits of a well-designed data warehouse are numerous. It provides a single source of truth for business intelligence, enabling consistent reporting and analysis across the organization. By integrating data from disparate sources, it eliminates data silos and provides a holistic view of the business. The historical data stored in the warehouse allows for trend analysis and forecasting, facilitating informed decision-making. Improved data quality, achieved through the ETL process, ensures accurate and reliable insights. Furthermore, by offloading analytical processing from operational systems, the data warehouse improves the performance of these systems, allowing them to focus on transactional processing.

Distinguishing a data warehouse from a data mart is crucial. While both serve analytical purposes, they differ in scope and focus. A data warehouse is an enterprise-wide repository containing data from multiple sources, providing a broad view of the entire organization. In contrast, a data mart is a smaller, specialized subset of the data warehouse, focusing on a specific department or business function, like sales, marketing, or finance. Data marts are designed to address the specific needs of individual departments, providing quicker access to relevant data. They are typically derived from the larger data warehouse, offering a more focused view of the data.

Another key concept related to data warehousing is online analytical processing (OLAP). OLAP enables users to analyze data from multiple dimensions, such as time, product, and region. It allows for complex calculations, aggregations, and drill-down analysis to uncover hidden trends and patterns. OLAP tools provide an interactive interface for exploring data and generating insightful reports. For instance, an analyst can use OLAP to analyze sales performance by product category, region, and time period, drilling down into specific areas of interest to understand sales patterns and identify potential growth opportunities. This multidimensional analysis capability sets OLAP apart from traditional querying tools, which are typically limited to two-dimensional analysis.

Finally, the Extract, Transform, Load (ETL) process is the backbone of data warehousing. ETL is the series of steps involved in extracting data from various source systems, transforming it into a consistent format suitable for analysis, and loading it into the data warehouse. This process involves data cleansing, standardization, and integration to ensure data quality and consistency. ETL tools automate this complex process, making it more efficient and reliable. They handle the complexities of data extraction from various sources, data transformation rules, and loading data into the target data warehouse. Understanding these core concepts—subject-orientation, integration, time-variance, non-volatility, data marts, OLAP, and ETL—is fundamental to grasping the power and potential of data warehousing for driving business intelligence. This foundational knowledge forms the basis for effective data warehouse design, implementation, and utilization. From this understanding, we can build robust and insightful analytical systems.

1.2 Key Concepts and Terminology

A data warehouse is a complex ecosystem with its own language. Understanding this terminology is crucial for navigating the complexities of data warehousing and effectively communicating with stakeholders. This chapter provides definitions of key terms and concepts, laying a solid foundation for subsequent chapters. We'll start with the core component: the data warehouse itself. It is a central repository of integrated data from one or more disparate sources. Its purpose is to support business intelligence (BI) and decision-making by providing a historical perspective of data, often referred to as a "single source of truth." Unlike operational databases designed for transactional processing, data warehouses are optimized for analytical queries.

Data marts represent a subset of a data warehouse focused on a specific department or business function like sales, marketing, or finance. They provide a more focused and often simplified view of data relevant to a particular team. Think of it like a mini data warehouse tailored to specific needs. This allows for quicker query responses and easier access to relevant information. While data warehouses offer a broad overview, data marts delve deeper into specific areas.

Extract, Transform, Load (ETL) is the process of extracting data from various sources, transforming it into a consistent format, and loading it into the data warehouse. This process is essential for ensuring data quality and consistency. ETL involves complex data manipulation and cleansing operations. These operations address inconsistencies, errors, and redundancies across different data sources. Imagine it as a refinery, converting raw data into a usable format for the data warehouse.

Online Analytical Processing (OLAP) refers to a category of software tools that enable multidimensional analysis of data stored in a data warehouse. OLAP allows users to analyze data from different perspectives, drill down into details, and perform complex calculations. It provides the ability to slice and dice data, enabling users to explore different aggregations and hierarchies. It empowers users to uncover hidden patterns and trends. Unlike traditional reporting, which often presents static data, OLAP facilitates interactive exploration and analysis.

A schema is a blueprint or structure that defines how data is organized within a database or data warehouse. It outlines the tables, columns, data types, and relationships between different data elements. A well-designed schema is essential for efficient data storage and retrieval. It enforces data integrity and consistency. Consider it as the architectural plan of the data warehouse. A robust schema allows for easy navigation and efficient analysis of the stored data.

Dimensional modeling is a data modeling technique specifically designed for data warehouses. It organizes data into fact tables and dimension tables. Fact tables contain numerical measures or facts, while dimension tables provide context to these facts. This structure allows for efficient querying and analysis of large datasets. Think of fact tables

as the 'what' and dimension tables as the 'who, what, when, where, and why.'
Star schema is the most common type of dimensional model. It consists of a central fact table surrounded by multiple dimension tables, resembling a star. This simple yet powerful structure facilitates easy understanding and querying of data. It provides a clear representation of relationships between facts and dimensions, enabling users to analyze data from various perspectives. The star schema is the bedrock of many successful data warehouse implementations.
Snowflake schema is a variation of the star schema where some dimension tables are normalized, meaning they are further broken down into smaller tables. This normalization reduces data redundancy but can increase query complexity. It offers a more granular level of detail compared to the star schema. The snowflake schema is chosen when data integrity and normalization are paramount, despite the increased complexity in querying.
Slowly Changing Dimensions (SCD) refer to techniques used to manage changes in dimension attributes over time. These changes can include corrections, updates, or additions. SCD Type 1 overwrites the previous value with the new one, effectively losing historical data. SCD Type 2 creates a new record with the updated value, preserving history. SCD Type 3 maintains both the current and previous values in the same record. Understanding these types is critical for maintaining data accuracy and tracking changes over time.
Data governance encompasses the policies, processes, and standards that ensure data quality, consistency, and security throughout the data warehouse lifecycle. It involves defining roles and responsibilities related to data management. Data governance ensures data accuracy, reliability, and compliance with regulatory requirements. A robust data governance framework is essential for building trust in the data warehouse and

ensuring its long-term success. It provides the guardrails for responsible data management.

Metadata refers to "data about data." In the context of a data warehouse, metadata describes the data stored within it, including its source, format, structure, and meaning. Metadata helps users understand the data and use it effectively. It facilitates data discovery, lineage tracking, and impact analysis. Think of it as a comprehensive guidebook to the data warehouse. Well-maintained metadata is crucial for navigating the complexities of a data warehouse and ensuring data quality.

1.3 Evolution of Data Warehousing

The earliest forms of data warehousing can be traced back to the late 1960s and the concept of "business intelligence." General Mills, seeking a way to analyze supermarket scanner data for improved marketing strategies, developed an early form of a decision support system. This pioneering effort highlighted the growing need to separate transactional systems, designed for daily operations, from analytical systems designed for complex querying and reporting. This distinction became crucial as businesses recognized the value of historical data for trend analysis and strategic decision-making. These early systems, however, were often cumbersome, expensive, and limited by the technology of the time.

The 1980s saw the emergence of the term "data warehouse" itself, largely attributed to IBM researchers Barry Devlin and Paul Murphy. They envisioned a system specifically designed to support business analysis, separating analytical processing from transactional systems to improve performance and data integrity. This period also saw the development of key concepts, such as the separation of operational and analytical systems, and the importance of data cleansing and transformation. The focus shifted from simply storing data to preparing and structuring it for effective analysis. This marked a significant step forward, though practical implementation remained challenging due to technological limitations and the complexities of integrating diverse data sources.

The 1990s ushered in a period of significant advancement, driven by the relational database management system (RDBMS) technology and the rise of Bill Inmon, often considered the "father of the data warehouse." Inmon's work formalized the concept of a data warehouse as a subject-oriented, integrated, time-variant, and non-volatile collection of data. This definition provided a clear framework for designing and building data warehouses. Ralph Kimball, another influential figure, championed dimensional modeling, a technique that structures data in a way optimized for business user understanding and query performance. These methodologies made data warehousing more accessible and practical for a wider range of organizations.

The early 2000s witnessed the proliferation of data warehousing appliances, pre-configured hardware and software systems designed specifically for data warehousing. These appliances offered improved performance and scalability compared to traditional RDBMS solutions, making it easier for organizations to handle growing data volumes. The rise of extract, transform, and load (ETL) tools streamlined the process of integrating data from various sources into the warehouse. This period saw a significant decrease in the cost and complexity of implementing data warehouses, leading to wider adoption across different industries.

The advent of cloud computing in the late 2000s and beyond revolutionized data warehousing. Cloud-based data warehouses offered flexibility, scalability, and cost-effectiveness, allowing organizations to quickly deploy and scale their data warehousing infrastructure without significant upfront investment. Providers like Amazon Web Services, Microsoft Azure, and Google Cloud Platform began offering cloud-based data warehousing solutions, further accelerating the adoption of cloud data warehousing. This shift also enabled new possibilities for real-time data warehousing and the integration of data warehouses with other big data technologies.

Today, the evolution continues with the rise of concepts like the data lake and the convergence of data warehousing and big data analytics. Data lakes, unlike structured data warehouses, store data in its raw format, offering greater flexibility for exploration and discovery. This complements the structured approach of traditional data warehousing, enabling organizations to combine structured and unstructured data for a more comprehensive view. The emergence of technologies like Hadoop and Spark has facilitated the processing of vast amounts of data, allowing organizations to derive deeper insights from their data assets.

Looking ahead, the future of data warehousing is likely to be shaped by several key trends. The increasing availability of real-time data and the demand for faster insights are driving the development of real-time data warehousing architectures. The continued growth of cloud computing and the emergence of serverless computing are further reducing the cost and complexity of deploying and managing data warehouses. Artificial intelligence and machine learning are also playing an increasing role in automating data integration, data quality management, and data analysis within the data warehousing context. This convergence of technologies promises to deliver even more powerful and accessible data warehousing solutions in the years to come. The evolution from simple decision support systems to complex cloud-based analytical platforms highlights the enduring importance of data-driven decision-making in the modern business landscape.

2 Chapter 2: Data Modeling for Warehouses

A well-structured data warehouse relies heavily on a robust data model. This model dictates how data is organized, accessed, and ultimately, how valuable it is for analysis. Within data warehousing, dimensional modeling has emerged as the dominant approach. It provides a clear, intuitive structure that simplifies complex data relationships and facilitates efficient querying. Think of it as the blueprint for your data warehouse. This framework is specifically tailored for analytical processing, unlike the normalized models commonly used in transactional systems.

Dimensional modeling revolves around two core components: fact tables and dimension tables. Fact tables are the heart of the model, storing the measurable facts or metrics of your business. These are the quantifiable data points you want to analyze, such as sales figures, website visits, or production output. Each row in a fact table represents a specific business event. Dimension tables, on the other hand, provide the context surrounding these facts. They contain descriptive attributes that categorize and enrich the data in the fact tables. Examples include product details, customer demographics, time periods, or geographical locations.

The relationship between fact and dimension tables is crucial. Fact tables are connected to dimension tables through foreign keys, creating a star-like structure, hence the term "star schema." This structure enables users to easily slice and dice data across various dimensions. Imagine analyzing sales figures by product category, region, and time period – the star schema makes these complex queries straightforward. More complex scenarios might involve multiple fact tables connected to shared dimension tables, forming a "snowflake schema." This structure offers greater normalization, potentially reducing redundancy, but can increase query complexity compared to the simpler star schema.

Schema design within a data warehouse requires careful consideration of various factors. The chosen schema significantly impacts query performance and data integrity. One key aspect is choosing the right level of granularity for your fact tables. Granularity refers to the level of detail captured in the data. For example, storing sales data at the individual transaction level provides high granularity, while summarizing sales by day offers lower granularity. Choosing the appropriate level of granularity depends on the specific analytical needs of your organization. Higher granularity offers greater flexibility but increases storage requirements and potentially impacts query performance. Conversely, lower granularity offers better query performance but reduces the level of detail available for analysis.

Data integrity is paramount in a data warehouse. Implementing proper constraints and data validation rules ensures the accuracy and consistency of your data. Primary keys uniquely identify records in dimension tables, while foreign keys enforce referential integrity between fact and dimension tables, preventing orphaned records. Data type selection plays a crucial role in both storage efficiency and query performance. Choosing appropriate data types, such as integer for numeric data and varchar for text data, optimizes storage space and improves the efficiency of data retrieval. Consider using smaller data types where possible, for example, using smallint instead of int if the range of values allows it.

Indexing is another critical aspect of schema design. Properly indexed columns significantly speed up query execution. Consider indexing frequently queried columns, particularly foreign keys that link fact and dimension tables. However, excessive indexing can negatively impact data loading performance. Finding the right balance is key to achieving optimal overall performance. Regularly analyze query patterns and adjust indexing strategies accordingly to maintain efficient data access.

Beyond technical considerations, the schema design should align with the business requirements. The model should reflect the key business processes and metrics that drive decision-making. Effective communication between data modelers and business users is essential to ensure the data warehouse meets the organization's analytical needs. Involve business stakeholders early in the design process to capture their requirements and validate the model's suitability for their intended use cases.

Understanding the intricacies of dimensional modeling and schema design empowers you to create a robust and efficient data warehouse. This foundation ensures your data is readily accessible and provides meaningful insights. By thoughtfully considering factors like granularity, data integrity, and indexing, you can create a data warehouse that truly serves as a powerful asset for your organization's analytical endeavors. This methodical approach to data modeling will ultimately contribute to better informed decisions and a more competitive edge in the marketplace.

2.1 Dimensional Modeling

At the heart of a well-designed data warehouse lies a robust data model. This chapter focuses on dimensional modeling, a widely adopted approach specifically tailored for analytical processing. Dimensional modeling simplifies complex data relationships, making it easier to understand, query, and analyze the information stored within a data warehouse. Its structure is designed to deliver optimal query performance for business intelligence and reporting, a critical aspect of deriving value from data.

Dimensional modeling revolves around two fundamental table types: fact tables and dimension tables. Fact tables represent the core measurements or "facts" of your business processes. These measurements could be sales figures, website clicks, production output, or any quantifiable metric relevant to your analytical needs. They are typically numeric and additive, meaning they can be aggregated across various dimensions. For instance, in a sales fact table, the 'sales amount' is a typical additive fact. You can sum it up to calculate total sales by product, region, or time period.

Dimension tables, on the other hand, provide the context surrounding these facts. They contain descriptive attributes that categorize and classify the facts. Common dimensions include time, product, customer, location, and employee. Imagine analyzing sales data; a product dimension table would hold details like product name, category, SKU, and manufacturer. Linking these descriptive attributes to the sales figures in the fact table allows analysts to slice and dice the data, gaining insights into sales performance across different product categories, brands, or individual products.

The relationship between fact and dimension tables is crucial. It is established through foreign keys in the fact table that reference primary keys in the dimension tables. This structure forms a star schema, where the fact table sits at the center, surrounded by radiating dimension tables. This schema simplifies queries, allowing for faster retrieval and aggregation of data compared to the complex, normalized schemas often used in operational databases. A variation, known as the snowflake schema, introduces normalized dimension tables, offering increased data integrity and reduced redundancy at the potential cost of slightly more complex queries due to the additional joins required.

Choosing between a star and snowflake schema depends on the specific requirements of the project, balancing query performance and data management considerations.

Designing effective dimension tables requires careful consideration of the business requirements. Each dimension table should be designed around a single business concept, ensuring clarity and ease of use. The granularity of a dimension table – the level of detail it represents – is another important design decision. For instance, a time dimension can be granular to the day, week, month, or year, depending on the reporting needs. Too much detail can lead to excessively large tables and impact query performance, while too little detail can limit the depth of analysis possible. Finding the right balance is key.

Slowly Changing Dimensions (SCDs) represent a vital aspect of dimensional modeling. They address the challenge of handling changes in dimension attributes over time. For example, a customer might change their address. How should this change be reflected in the data warehouse? There are several established SCD types, each with its own approach. Type 1 overwrites the old value with the new one, maintaining a single record for the customer. Type 2 creates a new record for the customer with the updated address, preserving the historical data. Type 3 maintains both the current and previous values within a single record. The choice of SCD type depends on the business requirements and the need to track historical changes.

Fact tables can be categorized based on the level of aggregation they represent. Transaction fact tables store individual transactions, such as every single sale. Periodic snapshot fact tables summarize data over a specific time period, like monthly sales totals. Accumulating snapshot fact tables track changes to a specific metric over time, such as the balance of a bank account. Understanding these different fact table types is crucial for designing a data model that efficiently supports various reporting requirements.

Additive facts, discussed earlier, are straightforward to aggregate. However, some facts are non-additive, such as ratios or percentages. These require special handling during aggregation and should be clearly identified in the data model. Semi-additive facts can be aggregated across some dimensions but not others. For example, account balances can be summed across customers but not across time. These nuances require careful consideration during design to ensure accurate reporting.

Dimensional modeling, while powerful, is not without its considerations. Data volume and complexity can impact performance, especially with very large fact tables. Careful design and indexing strategies are essential for optimizing query performance. Maintaining data consistency across dimensions can also be a challenge. Implementing robust data quality processes and ensuring consistent naming conventions are essential for a successful implementation. Lastly, the design should anticipate future reporting requirements. Building flexibility into the model allows it to accommodate evolving business needs without requiring significant rework.

2.2 Schema Design

A well-designed schema is the bedrock of a successful data warehouse. It dictates how data is organized, accessed, and ultimately, how effectively it can be used for analysis. This chapter will delve into the intricacies of schema design, focusing on practical techniques to create a robust and efficient structure. We'll explore various schema types, discuss the rationale behind choosing one over another, and examine the impact of design choices on query performance and scalability. This journey through schema design will equip you with the knowledge to construct a data warehouse that truly empowers your organization.

One common approach in data warehousing is the star schema. This design gets its name from its visual resemblance to a star, with a central fact table surrounded by radiating dimension tables. The fact table contains the measurable data, often numerical values like sales figures or website visits. Dimension tables, on the other hand, provide context to these facts. They contain descriptive attributes like product categories, customer demographics, or time periods. This structure simplifies querying by allowing users to easily filter and aggregate data based on specific dimensions. Imagine analyzing sales figures by product category and region. A star schema makes this task straightforward by providing direct links between the sales facts and the relevant product and region dimensions.

Another popular schema type is the snowflake schema. It builds upon the star schema by normalizing the dimension tables. Normalization involves breaking down tables into smaller, more granular units, reducing data redundancy and improving data integrity. While normalization can offer benefits in terms of storage efficiency and data consistency, it also adds complexity to queries. Accessing data now requires joining multiple tables, potentially impacting query performance. Choosing between a star and snowflake schema requires careful consideration of the trade-offs between query simplicity and data normalization. For instance, a rapidly growing data warehouse with limited storage capacity might benefit from the efficiencies of a snowflake schema, whereas a warehouse prioritizing rapid query response times might favor the simplicity of a star schema.

Beyond star and snowflake schemas, there are other specialized schema designs like the fact constellation schema. This schema, also known as a galaxy schema, connects multiple fact tables with shared dimension tables. It's particularly useful when dealing with multiple related business processes, allowing for a more integrated and holistic view of the data. Consider a retail business that wants to analyze both sales and inventory data. A fact constellation schema allows for both fact tables (sales and inventory) to share common dimension tables like product and time, enabling cross-process analysis. This structure allows for complex queries that span different facets of the business, providing deeper insights than isolated analyses.

No matter which schema type you choose, several key considerations will guide you toward an efficient and effective design. Firstly, understand your business requirements thoroughly. The schema should reflect the specific analytical needs of your organization. What questions do you need to answer? Which dimensions are most critical for analysis? Answering these questions will inform your design choices. Secondly, consider data volume and growth. A schema designed for a small dataset might not scale well as the data warehouse grows. Choosing a schema that can accommodate future data expansion is crucial for long-term success. Think about how data volume might impact query performance and storage requirements.

Performance optimization is another critical aspect of schema design. Techniques like indexing and partitioning can significantly improve query speeds. Indexing creates a lookup table that speeds up data retrieval, while partitioning divides the data into smaller, more manageable chunks. Both techniques contribute to faster query response times, especially for large datasets. Similarly, choosing the right data types for your attributes can also impact performance. Using smaller data types where possible can reduce storage space and improve query efficiency. Finally, data governance and maintainability are essential considerations. A well-designed schema should be easy to understand, maintain, and update. Proper documentation and naming conventions can significantly simplify these tasks. Regularly reviewing and refining the schema is crucial for maintaining its efficiency and relevance as business needs evolve. This ongoing maintenance ensures that the data warehouse remains a valuable asset for decision-making. By carefully considering these factors, you can create a schema that not only supports current analytical needs but also adapts to future demands, ensuring the long-term success of your data warehouse initiative.

3 Chapter 3: ETL Process Fundamentals

The journey of data from its raw state in various source systems to becoming valuable information within a data warehouse hinges on the Extract, Transform, Load (ETL) process. This process, a cornerstone of data warehousing, involves three distinct yet interconnected stages. Each stage plays a critical role in ensuring data accuracy, consistency, and usability for analytical reporting and business intelligence. Understanding the nuances of each stage is paramount for building a robust and effective data warehouse.

Extraction, the first step, involves retrieving data from a multitude of source systems. These sources can vary significantly, encompassing relational databases like Oracle and MySQL, NoSQL databases like MongoDB and Cassandra, flat files like CSV and text files, and even real-time data streams from applications and sensors. The extraction methods employed must be tailored to the specific characteristics of each source. For relational databases, direct SQL queries offer efficient data retrieval, allowing for targeted extraction based on specific criteria. For flat files, parsers are utilized to interpret the data structure and extract the relevant information. Real-time data streams often require specialized connectors or APIs to capture the continuous flow of data. The complexity of the extraction process often depends on the heterogeneity and volume of the source systems.

Transformation, the second stage, focuses on converting the extracted data into a consistent and standardized format suitable for the data warehouse. This crucial step addresses data quality issues, inconsistencies, and redundancies that may exist in the source data. Data cleansing techniques, such as removing duplicates, handling missing values, and correcting errors, are employed to enhance data accuracy. Data standardization involves transforming data into a uniform format, ensuring consistency across all sources. For example, date formats, units of measurement, and currency values are standardized to eliminate discrepancies. Data enrichment can also be performed during this stage, incorporating data from external sources to enhance the analytical value of the data warehouse. This might involve appending geographic information based on customer addresses or integrating social media sentiment analysis. The transformation stage often requires complex data manipulation logic and careful consideration of business rules.

The final stage, loading, involves transferring the transformed data into the target data warehouse. The loading process must be optimized for performance, especially when dealing with large volumes of data. Different loading strategies exist, each with its own advantages and disadvantages. Full loading involves replacing the entire target table with the new data, while incremental loading appends only new or changed data. Choosing the appropriate loading strategy depends on the frequency of data updates, the size of the data, and the desired data warehouse refresh cycle. Data validation checks are implemented during the loading process to ensure the integrity and accuracy of the loaded data. This might involve comparing record counts, validating data types, and checking for data consistency. The loading process concludes the ETL cycle, making the data available for analysis and reporting.

Managing data quality throughout the ETL process is paramount for building a reliable and trustworthy data warehouse. Data quality checks are implemented at each stage to identify and address potential issues. Data profiling techniques help understand the characteristics and distribution of data in the source systems. Data validation rules ensure data accuracy and consistency during the transformation stage. Data cleansing processes address inconsistencies and errors in the source data. Continuous monitoring of data quality metrics, such as data completeness, accuracy, and timeliness, is essential for maintaining a high level of data quality. Implementing a robust data quality management framework throughout the ETL process ensures that the data warehouse provides accurate and reliable insights for decision-making.

Various ETL tools and technologies exist to streamline and automate the ETL process. These tools offer a range of functionalities, including data extraction from diverse sources, data transformation capabilities, data quality management features, and data loading into target systems. Popular ETL tools include Informatica PowerCenter, Talend Open Studio, and Apache Kafka. Choosing the right ETL tool depends on the specific requirements of the data warehouse project, considering factors such as data volume, data complexity, and budget constraints. These tools offer pre-built connectors for various source systems, simplifying the extraction process. They also provide graphical interfaces for designing and managing ETL workflows, reducing the need for manual coding. By leveraging the capabilities of these tools, organizations can efficiently and effectively manage the complex ETL process, ensuring the timely and accurate delivery of data to the data warehouse. The selection of appropriate tools is a key consideration in the design and implementation of any data warehousing solution. Properly utilized, these tools contribute significantly to the overall efficiency and effectiveness of the data warehousing process.

3.1 Extraction Techniques

The bedrock of any successful data warehouse lies in the efficient and reliable extraction of data from its source systems. These sources can be incredibly diverse, ranging from traditional relational databases like Oracle and SQL Server to NoSQL databases like MongoDB and Cassandra, flat files like CSV and Excel spreadsheets, and even real-time data streams from applications and sensors. Understanding the nuances of each source type and applying appropriate extraction techniques is crucial for building a robust and accurate data warehouse.

Let's begin by examining extraction from relational databases. This often involves using SQL queries to select the required data based on specific criteria. Incremental extraction, capturing only changes since the last extraction, is a common practice to minimize load on source systems and improve efficiency. Techniques like change data capture (CDC) and timestamp-based extraction can be employed to achieve this. Understanding the underlying database schema and optimizing queries for performance are essential for successful extraction. Considerations like minimizing the impact on operational systems during peak hours should also be factored in.

Moving on to NoSQL databases, the extraction process differs significantly due to their schema-less nature. While some NoSQL databases support SQL-like query languages, others rely on APIs or specialized drivers for data access. Understanding the data model and query language of the specific NoSQL database is paramount. Exporting data to a staging area in a structured format, like JSON or CSV, before loading into the data warehouse is often a practical approach.

Flat files, while seemingly simple, can present their own set of challenges. Data inconsistencies, varying delimiters, and differing header formats require careful handling. Parsing techniques and data validation rules must be implemented to ensure data quality and consistency. Tools and scripting languages like Python can be invaluable for automating the extraction and pre-processing of data from flat files. It's important to thoroughly understand the structure and format of these files before attempting extraction, often requiring careful inspection and documentation.

Extracting from real-time data streams requires a different approach altogether. Message queues like Kafka and Amazon SQS, and streaming platforms like Apache Flink and Spark Streaming, are commonly used to capture and process real-time data. These technologies allow for continuous data ingestion and processing, enabling near real-time updates to the data warehouse. Understanding the specific API and message format of the streaming platform is crucial for seamless integration. Furthermore, handling potential data velocity spikes and ensuring data integrity during high-volume streaming are important considerations.

Another important source for data warehousing is application programming interfaces (APIs). Many applications expose data through well-defined APIs, allowing for programmatic access. Understanding the API documentation and authentication mechanisms is crucial for successful extraction. Rate limiting, pagination, and error handling are important aspects to consider when interacting with APIs. Tools like Postman can be used to explore and test APIs before implementing the extraction process. Choosing the right API extraction method, be it a direct connection, a dedicated connector, or building custom scripts, depends on the specific API and the data warehouse architecture.

Web scraping, the process of extracting data from websites, can also be a valuable source, especially for competitive intelligence or market research. However, ethical and legal

considerations, such as respecting robots.txt and terms of service, are paramount. Using appropriate libraries and tools for web scraping, while adhering to website guidelines, is essential for responsible data acquisition. Navigating website structures, handling dynamic content, and managing pagination are key challenges in web scraping.
Finally, legacy systems, often characterized by outdated technologies and complex data structures, can pose significant extraction challenges. Reverse engineering data formats, understanding proprietary interfaces, and working with limited documentation can be a tedious process. Sometimes, collaborating with individuals who have historical knowledge of the legacy system can be crucial for successful extraction. Developing customized extraction scripts or utilizing specialized data migration tools can be necessary for integrating data from legacy systems.
Regardless of the source, metadata management plays a vital role in successful extraction. Documenting data sources, data lineage, and transformation rules ensures data quality and traceability. Maintaining a comprehensive metadata repository provides a valuable resource for understanding the data within the data warehouse. This is especially important for regulatory compliance and auditing purposes.
In conclusion, mastering data extraction is an essential skill for any data warehousing professional. Choosing the right techniques for each source, understanding the data structures, implementing robust error handling, and maintaining proper metadata are crucial for building a reliable and efficient data warehouse that provides actionable insights. By carefully considering these various aspects, data warehouse architects can ensure that their ETL processes are robust, efficient, and capable of handling the diverse data landscape of modern businesses.

3.2 Transformation Strategies

Data transformation is the crucial bridge connecting raw data from various sources to the meticulously structured environment of a data warehouse. It's where the raw materials are refined, reshaped, and prepared for meaningful analysis. This process involves a series of carefully orchestrated steps, each designed to address specific challenges and requirements. One primary goal is data cleansing. This involves identifying and rectifying inconsistencies, errors, and inaccuracies. Think of it as meticulously polishing a gem, removing imperfections to reveal its true brilliance. Strategies for cleansing might include handling missing values, correcting data entry mistakes, and removing duplicate records. Imagine a dataset with inconsistent customer addresses; transformation would standardize these entries, ensuring uniformity and accuracy for marketing campaigns or logistical planning.

Data type conversion is another fundamental aspect of transformation. This involves changing the format of data to ensure compatibility and consistency within the warehouse. For instance, dates might be stored in various formats across different source systems. Transformations standardize these to a single, consistent format for accurate temporal analysis. Similarly, numerical data might need to be converted from text strings to numerical formats for calculations and aggregations. Consider sales data recorded as text; transformation converts it to numerical values, enabling calculations of total revenue or average transaction value. Without such conversions, meaningful analysis becomes impossible.

Data integration is a crucial step, combining data from disparate sources into a unified structure. This often involves complex mappings and transformations to reconcile differing data definitions and structures. Imagine merging customer data from an online store with data from a physical retail location. Transformation aligns these datasets, creating a single, comprehensive view of each customer. This unified view provides a richer understanding of customer behavior, enabling more targeted marketing efforts and improved customer service. The integration process can also involve data deduplication and resolution of conflicting information, ensuring the integrity and reliability of the combined data.

Data reduction is another critical aspect of transformation, particularly when dealing with massive datasets. This involves reducing the volume of data without sacrificing essential information. Techniques like aggregation, summarization, and filtering are used to create a more manageable and efficient dataset for analysis. For instance, instead of storing every individual transaction, daily sales totals might suffice for certain analyses. This reduces storage costs and improves query performance without significant information loss. Data reduction strategies must be carefully chosen to avoid discarding valuable insights while maximizing efficiency.

Data derivation and enrichment involve creating new data elements based on existing ones or adding external data to enhance the warehouse. This adds context and depth to the existing data, allowing for richer analysis. Calculating profit margins from revenue and cost data is an example of data derivation. Enriching customer data with demographic information from third-party sources adds another layer of understanding. Imagine adding geographic location data to customer profiles, enabling regional sales analysis and targeted marketing campaigns. This enriched data provides valuable insights that would be unavailable with the original data alone. Deriving new attributes and enriching data expands the analytical possibilities, revealing hidden patterns and trends.

Finally, consider data encryption and masking for sensitive information. This is crucial for maintaining data security and privacy compliance. Encrypting sensitive data protects it from unauthorized access, while masking techniques obscure confidential information during testing and development. Imagine masking credit card numbers while retaining the last four digits for identification purposes. This protects sensitive data while still allowing for necessary analysis and development activities. Implementing these security measures ensures compliance with regulations and safeguards sensitive information from unauthorized access and misuse. Data security is paramount, and transformation plays a key role in protecting sensitive data within the warehouse.

3.3 Loading Data into the Warehouse

The efficient movement of data from disparate sources into your warehouse is the crux of a successful data warehousing strategy. This process, the "loading" phase of ETL, encompasses several key considerations: choosing the right loading method, optimizing performance, and ensuring data integrity. A poorly executed load process can lead to data inconsistencies, performance bottlenecks, and ultimately, compromised insights. Understanding the nuances of various loading techniques is therefore essential.

Let's explore the primary loading methods: full loads, incremental loads, and delta loads. A full load involves replacing the entire target table with fresh data. This approach, while straightforward, becomes increasingly cumbersome and resource-intensive as data volumes grow. It's best suited for initial data population or situations where historical data needs a complete refresh. Imagine setting up your warehouse for the first time; a full load is often the most practical starting point.

Incremental loads, on the other hand, offer a more efficient approach by only adding new or changed data to the target table. This significantly reduces processing time and resource consumption, particularly beneficial for large data warehouses. Consider a scenario where you receive daily sales transactions. Instead of reloading all sales data every day, an incremental load appends only the new transactions, preserving existing data. Delta loads take incremental loading a step further by identifying and loading only the changes within existing data. This requires a robust change data capture (CDC) mechanism to track modifications at the source. Think of a product catalog where only a few attributes, such as price or availability, are updated regularly. A delta load would pinpoint and update only those specific attributes, offering maximum efficiency.

Choosing the appropriate loading method depends on various factors, including data volume, frequency of updates, and the nature of the source systems. For instance, a system with frequent, small changes might benefit from incremental or delta loads, while a system with infrequent, large changes might be better served by periodic full loads. There's no one-size-fits-all solution; careful evaluation of your specific needs is crucial.

Beyond choosing the right method, optimizing load performance is paramount. Several techniques can significantly improve loading speed and efficiency. Partitioning large tables can dramatically reduce the time required for loading and querying by dividing the data into smaller, more manageable chunks. Think of it like organizing a vast library into separate sections for different genres. Similarly, indexing key columns can accelerate data retrieval during the loading process.

Data quality checks are also an integral part of the loading process. Validating data types, enforcing data integrity constraints, and handling duplicates ensure the accuracy and reliability of the loaded data. Imagine loading sales data with incorrect date formats or duplicate customer records. Such errors can lead to flawed reports and unreliable insights. Implementing data quality checks during the load process helps prevent these issues and maintains the integrity of your warehouse.

Furthermore, consider the specific requirements of your target data warehouse environment. Different database systems have their own nuances and optimizations for data loading. Understanding these specifics can significantly impact performance. For example, bulk loading utilities, offered by many database systems, are designed for high-volume data imports and can significantly outperform standard insert statements. Similarly, utilizing staging tables within the warehouse can provide a temporary holding area for data transformations and cleansing before the final load into the target tables. Finally, effective monitoring and logging are crucial for identifying and resolving any issues during the load process. Detailed logs provide valuable information about loading times, errors encountered, and data volumes processed. This information can be used to pinpoint bottlenecks, optimize performance, and ensure the overall health of the loading process. Imagine a scenario where a load process unexpectedly fails. Detailed logs can help quickly identify the root cause and implement corrective actions, minimizing downtime and ensuring data consistency. Therefore, implementing robust monitoring and logging procedures is an essential aspect of a well-managed data warehouse.

By carefully considering these aspects – choosing the appropriate loading method, optimizing performance, ensuring data quality, understanding the target environment, and implementing monitoring – you can ensure a smooth, efficient, and reliable data loading process, setting the stage for effective analysis and actionable insights. Remember, the loading phase is not merely a technical task; it's a strategic imperative for building a successful data warehouse.

3.4 Data Quality Management

Ensuring high-quality data within your data warehouse is paramount to its success. A warehouse brimming with inaccurate, inconsistent, or incomplete data renders any analysis misleading, ultimately hindering decision-making. Think of it like building a house on a shaky foundation – it's only a matter of time before cracks appear. This chapter delves into the crucial aspects of data quality management within the ETL process, providing a framework for establishing and maintaining trust in your data.

Data quality issues can manifest in various forms, each with its own set of consequences. Duplicate records can skew aggregations and lead to inflated metrics. Inconsistent formatting across different data sources makes comparisons difficult and can lead to erroneous conclusions. Missing values, another common problem, can create gaps in analysis and limit the scope of insights. Imagine trying to analyze customer behavior without complete purchase history data – the resulting picture would be incomplete and potentially inaccurate.

A proactive approach to data quality involves implementing checks and balances throughout the ETL pipeline. Profiling, a critical first step, involves analyzing source data to understand its characteristics, identify potential issues, and establish a baseline for quality. This includes examining data distributions, identifying outliers, and checking for inconsistencies in data types and formats. Think of it as a health check for your data, providing a clear picture of its current state.

Cleansing, the next stage, tackles the identified data quality problems. This might involve standardizing formats, deduplicating records, handling missing values through imputation or removal, and correcting inconsistencies. Data cleansing transforms raw data into a reliable and usable form, ready for loading into the warehouse. It's like refining crude oil into gasoline – a necessary process to extract maximum value.

Validation rules play a vital role in ensuring ongoing data quality. These rules define acceptable ranges, formats, and relationships within the data, acting as gatekeepers to prevent bad data from entering the warehouse. For example, a validation rule might specify that customer ages must be positive and within a reasonable range, or that product IDs must match existing entries in a product master table. Such rules ensure that the data loaded into the warehouse adheres to predefined standards, maintaining its integrity over time.

Monitoring data quality metrics provides continuous feedback on the effectiveness of your data quality management efforts. Tracking metrics like the number of duplicates detected, the percentage of missing values, and the number of validation rule violations provides insights into the health of your data and alerts you to potential problems. Regularly reviewing these metrics allows you to identify trends, pinpoint areas for improvement, and adapt your data quality processes accordingly. This continuous monitoring acts as an early warning system, preventing small issues from escalating into major problems.

Establishing clear data quality rules and responsibilities is essential for a successful data quality program. Defining who is responsible for data quality at each stage of the ETL process ensures accountability and ownership. This could involve assigning data stewards to oversee specific data domains, empowering them to define data quality rules, monitor compliance, and address any data quality issues that arise. Clear roles and responsibilities foster a culture of data quality within the organization.

Documentation plays a critical role in maintaining data quality over time. Documenting data quality rules, processes, and metrics provides a valuable resource for new team members and ensures consistency in data quality management practices. A well-documented data quality program makes it easier to understand the rationale behind specific rules, track changes over time, and maintain a consistent approach to data quality across the organization. This documentation serves as a living guide for your data quality efforts.

Communicating data quality issues and resolutions effectively is essential for maintaining trust in the data. Regularly reporting on data quality metrics to stakeholders keeps them informed about the state of the data and demonstrates your commitment to data quality. Communicating about resolved data quality issues, along with the steps taken to prevent recurrence, helps build confidence in the data and reinforces the importance of data quality. Open communication fosters transparency and collaboration, building trust in the data and the insights derived from it.

Investing in data quality training for your team empowers them to identify and address data quality issues effectively. Training programs can cover topics such as data profiling techniques, data cleansing methods, validation rule development, and data quality monitoring. By equipping your team with the necessary skills and knowledge, you create a culture of data quality and ensure that everyone understands their role in maintaining data integrity. A well-trained team forms the backbone of a successful data quality program.

Implementing robust data quality management practices is an ongoing process, requiring continuous refinement and adaptation. As your data warehouse evolves and new data sources are integrated, it's crucial to revisit and update your data quality rules, processes, and metrics. Staying vigilant about data quality ensures that your data warehouse remains a reliable source of insights, enabling informed decision-making and driving business success. Data quality is not a destination, but a journey – a continuous effort to ensure the accuracy, consistency, and completeness of your data.

3.5 ETL Tools and Technologies

The Extract, Transform, Load (ETL) process forms the backbone of any successful data warehouse. Choosing the right tools and technologies for this process is critical. A robust ETL framework ensures data is accurately extracted from various sources, transformed into a usable format, and loaded efficiently into the data warehouse. This chapter will explore a range of popular ETL tools and technologies, outlining their strengths and weaknesses to help you make informed decisions for your data warehousing needs.

Traditional ETL tools like Informatica PowerCenter have long been industry staples. Known for its comprehensive features and scalability, PowerCenter provides a visual development environment for creating complex ETL workflows. Its robust data integration capabilities allow it to handle large volumes of data from diverse sources. However, the licensing costs can be substantial, making it a more suitable choice for enterprise-level projects. For organizations with tighter budgets, open-source alternatives like Talend Open Studio offer similar functionalities with the advantage of community support and cost-effectiveness. Talend's user-friendly interface and extensive library of pre-built components make it a compelling option for smaller teams and projects.

Beyond traditional ETL tools, scripting languages like Python are increasingly popular for data transformation tasks. Libraries such as Pandas and NumPy offer powerful data manipulation capabilities, allowing developers to write custom scripts for specific transformation needs. This approach provides greater flexibility and control compared to visual ETL tools, especially when dealing with complex transformations or unstructured data. Python's versatility extends to data extraction as well, with libraries that can connect to various databases, APIs, and file formats. While Python offers significant advantages in terms of flexibility and cost, it requires coding expertise and may lack the visual interface and pre-built components found in dedicated ETL tools.

Cloud-based ETL services have revolutionized the data warehousing landscape, providing scalable and cost-effective solutions for data integration. Services like AWS Glue and Azure Data Factory offer a serverless approach to ETL, eliminating the need for managing infrastructure. These services integrate seamlessly with other cloud offerings, simplifying data ingestion from various sources. Their pay-as-you-go pricing model makes them attractive for organizations looking to avoid upfront investments. While cloud-based ETL solutions offer significant advantages in terms of scalability and ease of use, considerations such as data security and vendor lock-in should be carefully evaluated.

Data virtualization tools offer a different approach to ETL, enabling access to data from disparate sources without requiring physical movement. Tools like Denodo create a virtual layer that integrates data from different systems, allowing users to query and analyze data in real-time. This approach eliminates the need for lengthy ETL processes and reduces data redundancy. Data virtualization is particularly useful for scenarios requiring real-time data access or integration of sensitive data that cannot be easily replicated. However, performance can be a concern when dealing with complex queries or large datasets, as the data is accessed and transformed on demand.

Choosing the right ETL approach depends on factors such as data volume, complexity, budget, and the technical expertise available within your organization. For large-scale enterprise data warehouses with complex transformations, traditional ETL tools like Informatica PowerCenter or open-source alternatives like Talend offer comprehensive capabilities and scalability. For smaller projects or organizations with coding expertise, scripting languages like Python provide greater flexibility and control. Cloud-based ETL services are ideal for organizations seeking scalability, cost-effectiveness, and seamless integration with cloud environments. Finally, data virtualization offers a powerful solution for real-time data access and integration of sensitive data.

Understanding the strengths and limitations of each approach is crucial for selecting the right tools and technologies for your specific needs. A well-designed ETL process, implemented with the right tools, ensures data accuracy, consistency, and timeliness, which are fundamental to building a successful data warehouse that delivers actionable insights. The ability to adapt to evolving data sources and business requirements further emphasizes the importance of selecting flexible and scalable ETL solutions. Carefully considering these factors will ensure your data warehouse project meets its objectives and provides the foundation for data-driven decision making. Therefore, take the time to evaluate your options and select the ETL approach that best aligns with your organization's resources and strategic goals. Remember, the right tools and technologies are critical to building a robust and efficient data warehouse.

4 Chapter 4: Data Storage and Management

Choosing the right storage architecture is fundamental to a successful data warehouse. Your choice will directly impact performance, scalability, and cost. Let's consider the dominant architectures: relational databases, columnar databases, and NoSQL solutions. Relational databases, the traditional choice, store data in rows and tables linked by relationships. This structure works well for transactional systems but can be less efficient for analytical queries typical in data warehousing. They excel at maintaining data integrity and consistency with ACID properties (Atomicity, Consistency, Isolation, Durability). However, complex analytical queries across multiple tables can lead to performance bottlenecks. Think of retrieving sales data for a specific product category across several regions; the database needs to scan multiple rows across potentially large tables.

Columnar databases, on the other hand, store data in columns rather than rows. This seemingly simple difference has profound implications for analytical queries. Imagine the same query for sales data. A columnar database can directly access and process only the relevant columns (product category, region, sales figures) without reading entire rows, leading to significantly faster query performance. This is particularly beneficial for aggregate functions like SUM and AVG. Furthermore, columnar storage lends itself well to compression, further improving storage efficiency and query speed. This advantage comes at a cost. Writing data to a columnar database can be slower than relational systems due to the need to write entire columns at a time.

NoSQL databases offer a more flexible approach to data storage. Unlike the structured schemas of relational and columnar databases, NoSQL systems can handle unstructured or semi-structured data, making them suitable for diverse data types like social media feeds, sensor data, or log files. This flexibility allows for faster development cycles and easier adaptation to evolving data requirements. Within NoSQL, there are different models like document stores, key-value stores, and graph databases, each catering to specific data structures and access patterns. Choosing the right NoSQL model requires careful consideration of your data characteristics and analytical needs. A document store might be ideal for storing customer profiles with varying attributes, while a key-value store suits simple lookups based on unique identifiers.

Data compression plays a crucial role in optimizing storage space and query performance in a data warehouse. By reducing the physical size of data, compression minimizes storage costs and the amount of data that needs to be read during query processing. Several compression techniques are commonly employed in data warehousing. Dictionary encoding replaces frequently occurring values with shorter codes. Imagine a large dataset with repeated city names. Dictionary encoding would create a lookup table where each city is assigned a unique code, reducing the storage footprint significantly. Run-length encoding compresses repeating sequences of values by storing the value and the number of times it repeats. This is effective for data with long sequences of identical values, like a series of sensor readings reporting the same temperature.

Bit-packing efficiently stores data by using the minimum number of bits required. For example, if a field only requires values between 0 and 63, it can be stored using only 6 bits instead of a full byte (8 bits). This seemingly small optimization can accumulate significant savings across large datasets. Delta encoding stores only the difference between consecutive values instead of the full values. This is particularly effective for time-series data where successive values often exhibit minimal change. Imagine tracking daily stock prices. Instead of storing the full price each day, delta encoding stores only the daily price change, resulting in smaller data sizes.

Choosing the right compression algorithm depends on the characteristics of the data and the query patterns. Highly repetitive data benefits from dictionary or run-length encoding, while numerical data with small variations can leverage bit-packing or delta encoding. Modern data warehousing solutions often employ a combination of these techniques to achieve optimal compression ratios. Furthermore, consider the trade-off between compression ratio and decompression speed. Higher compression ratios can lead to slower query performance due to the overhead of decompression. Balancing these factors is crucial for designing an efficient data storage strategy. Regularly evaluate your compression strategies as your data volume and query patterns evolve. Technological advancements constantly introduce new compression algorithms and techniques that might offer better performance or storage efficiency.

4.1 Storage Architectures

The physical organization of your data warehouse profoundly impacts its performance, scalability, and cost-effectiveness. Choosing the right architecture is a critical decision, influenced by factors like data volume, query complexity, budget, and the technical expertise available within your team. Let's examine several popular storage architectures, exploring their strengths and weaknesses.

Relational Database Management Systems (RDBMS) have long been a cornerstone of data warehousing. They offer mature technology, robust transaction management, and ACID properties (Atomicity, Consistency, Isolation, Durability), ensuring data integrity. RDBMS systems excel at handling structured data and complex joins, making them suitable for traditional data warehousing scenarios. However, they can struggle with massive datasets and complex analytical queries, often exhibiting performance bottlenecks as data volume grows. Popular examples include Oracle, SQL Server, PostgreSQL, and MySQL. Each system offers specific features and optimizations for data warehousing workloads, like partitioning and indexing strategies, that can significantly improve performance.

Columnar databases, in contrast to traditional row-oriented databases, store data by columns rather than rows. This organization is highly efficient for analytical queries that typically access only a subset of columns. By reading only the necessary data, columnar databases dramatically reduce I/O operations, leading to faster query performance, especially for aggregation and filtering operations. This architecture also lends itself well to compression techniques, further optimizing storage space and query speed. Examples of columnar databases include Vertica, Amazon Redshift, and ClickHouse. They are particularly well-suited for large-scale data warehousing where analytical performance is paramount.

Data appliances offer a pre-configured, integrated solution that combines hardware and software optimized for data warehousing. These appliances typically leverage massively parallel processing (MPP) architectures to distribute data and queries across multiple nodes, enabling high performance for complex analytical workloads. Data appliances simplify deployment and management compared to building a data warehouse from scratch. However, they can be more expensive than other solutions. Netezza, Teradata, and Exasol are examples of data appliances, each offering different features and capabilities catering to various data warehousing needs. They are often chosen by organizations with large data volumes and demanding performance requirements.

NoSQL databases provide a flexible schema-less approach to data storage. They are well-suited for handling semi-structured and unstructured data, like JSON and XML, which are increasingly common in modern data warehousing environments. NoSQL databases offer high scalability and availability, making them ideal for handling large volumes of rapidly changing data. Several types of NoSQL databases exist, including document stores (MongoDB, Couchbase), key-value stores (Redis, Amazon DynamoDB), and graph databases (Neo4j, Amazon Neptune). Each type excels in different use cases. When choosing a NoSQL database for your data warehouse, consider the specific data types and query patterns you will be working with. NoSQL databases can complement or even replace traditional relational databases in certain data warehousing scenarios.

Cloud-based data warehouses leverage the scalability and elasticity of cloud computing platforms to provide on-demand data warehousing capabilities. These services offer pay-as-you-go pricing models, reducing upfront infrastructure costs and allowing for easy scaling of resources based on demand. Cloud providers offer various managed services like Snowflake, Amazon Redshift, Google BigQuery, and Azure Synapse Analytics, which abstract away much of the complexity of managing a data warehouse. These services often incorporate advanced features like automatic scaling, data sharing, and built-in security. They are an increasingly popular choice for organizations of all sizes looking for a cost-effective and scalable data warehousing solution.

Hybrid architectures combine different storage technologies to leverage the strengths of each. For example, you might use a relational database for structured transactional data, a columnar database for analytical processing, and a NoSQL database for unstructured data. This approach allows for greater flexibility and optimization, but it requires careful planning and integration to ensure data consistency and efficient query performance across different systems. Designing a hybrid architecture necessitates a deep understanding of the different technologies involved and their respective strengths and weaknesses.

Selecting the optimal storage architecture requires a comprehensive assessment of your specific needs and priorities. Consider factors like data volume and velocity, query complexity, budget constraints, existing infrastructure, and the technical expertise of your team. Thorough testing and benchmarking are crucial to validate your chosen architecture and ensure it meets your performance and scalability requirements. Regularly evaluate your architecture as your data and business needs evolve. The data warehousing landscape is constantly evolving, with new technologies and approaches emerging regularly. Stay informed about the latest advancements to make informed decisions about your data warehouse architecture.

4.2 Data Compression

Efficient storage is a critical aspect of data warehousing, directly impacting both cost and performance. Therefore, understanding the principles and techniques of data compression is essential for building a successful data warehouse. Data compression involves encoding information using fewer bits than the original representation. This reduction in size not only saves valuable storage space but also leads to faster data retrieval and processing times, as less data needs to be read from disk or transferred across the network. Choosing the right compression method depends on factors such as the type of data being stored, desired compression ratio, and the trade-off between compression speed and decompression speed.

Several categories of compression algorithms exist, each with its own strengths and weaknesses. Lossless compression algorithms guarantee that the original data can be perfectly reconstructed from the compressed version. These methods are crucial for data warehousing where data integrity is paramount. Common lossless algorithms include run-length encoding (RLE), which efficiently compresses repetitive sequences, and dictionary-based methods like Lempel-Ziv (LZ) compression, which create a dictionary of frequently occurring patterns and replace them with shorter codes. Huffman coding, another lossless technique, assigns shorter codes to more frequent characters, further optimizing storage.

Lossy compression algorithms, on the other hand, achieve higher compression ratios by discarding some data during the compression process. While this approach is suitable for multimedia applications where a minor loss of fidelity is acceptable, it is generally not recommended for data warehousing where accuracy is critical. Imagine losing crucial decimal points in financial figures or misrepresenting customer demographics due to data loss. The consequences can be significant, leading to inaccurate analysis and flawed business decisions. Therefore, the focus in data warehousing remains firmly on lossless compression methods.

Choosing the appropriate compression technique depends heavily on the specific data characteristics within the warehouse. For example, data with high redundancy, such as long strings of identical characters, benefits greatly from run-length encoding. Textual data, often containing recurring phrases and words, is well-suited to dictionary-based methods like Lempel-Ziv compression. Furthermore, consider the nature of the data itself. Fact tables, typically containing numerical values, may benefit from different compression algorithms compared to dimension tables, which often store textual attributes. Analyzing the distribution and characteristics of your data is crucial in selecting the most effective compression strategy.

Modern data warehouse systems often offer built-in compression capabilities, allowing you to specify the desired algorithm and level of compression. Columnar databases, in particular, excel at compression because they store data by column rather than by row. This arrangement allows for more efficient compression within each column, as similar data types are grouped together. For example, a column containing customer ages can be compressed more effectively than a row containing a mixture of data types like age, name, and address. The ability to apply different compression algorithms to different columns further enhances storage efficiency. A column containing primarily textual data could be compressed using dictionary-based methods, while a column containing numerical data could be compressed using a different algorithm optimized for numbers.

Beyond choosing the right algorithm, consider the trade-off between compression and decompression speed. Higher compression ratios may come at the cost of slower decompression times. In a high-performance data warehouse where query response time is critical, a slightly lower compression ratio with faster decompression might be preferable. Furthermore, evaluate the computational resources required for compression and decompression. Some algorithms are more computationally intensive than others. Balancing compression efficiency with processing overhead is essential for maintaining optimal warehouse performance.

Effective data compression within your data warehouse is a key factor in optimizing storage space and query performance. By understanding the different compression algorithms and choosing the right technique based on your data characteristics, you can significantly reduce storage costs and improve the overall efficiency of your data warehouse. Remember that while achieving high compression ratios is desirable, maintaining data integrity is paramount. Focus on lossless compression methods to ensure that your analytical insights remain accurate and reliable. Finally, consider the trade-off between compression/decompression speed and computational resources when selecting a compression strategy. By carefully considering these factors, you can implement a robust data compression strategy that contributes significantly to the success of your data warehousing initiatives.

5 Chapter 5: Data Retrieval and Querying

Efficient data retrieval is the cornerstone of a successful data warehouse. After investing time and resources in building a robust data warehouse, the ability to quickly and accurately access information is paramount. This chapter will delve into the various methods and techniques for retrieving and querying data, empowering you to transform raw data into actionable insights. We'll explore the nuances of SQL, the power of OLAP and MDX, and the crucial role of performance tuning. Finally, we'll examine the tools and techniques for visualizing your data and creating compelling reports.

Structured Query Language (SQL) remains the workhorse for interacting with relational data warehouses. While familiar to most data professionals, its application in a data warehousing context requires specific considerations. Unlike operational databases optimized for transactional speed, data warehouses prioritize analytical queries that often involve aggregations, joins across large tables, and complex filtering. Therefore, understanding how to write efficient SQL queries is critical. This involves leveraging techniques like indexing, partitioning, and query optimization strategies specific to your chosen database platform. Moreover, understanding the underlying data model, particularly the relationships between fact and dimension tables, is crucial for crafting effective queries. For instance, retrieving sales data by product category requires joining the sales fact table with the product dimension table.

Online Analytical Processing (OLAP) and Multidimensional Expressions (MDX) provide powerful tools for analyzing data from multiple perspectives. OLAP allows users to explore data through a multidimensional lens, slicing and dicing information along different dimensions. For example, you can analyze sales figures by region, product, and time period simultaneously. MDX, a query language specifically designed for OLAP cubes, enables sophisticated calculations and aggregations within these multidimensional structures. While MDX might have a steeper learning curve than SQL, its ability to handle complex analytical queries makes it invaluable for data warehousing. Learning MDX involves understanding the concepts of cubes, dimensions, hierarchies, and members, and how to construct queries that navigate these structures effectively. Mastering MDX opens up a world of analytical possibilities, enabling you to extract deeper insights from your data.

Performance tuning plays a crucial role in ensuring timely data retrieval. A well-designed query can still perform poorly if the underlying infrastructure isn't optimized. This involves various techniques, including indexing, partitioning, and materialized views. Indexing speeds up data retrieval by creating lookup tables that point to the location of specific data. Partitioning divides large tables into smaller, more manageable chunks, enabling queries to target specific segments of the data. Materialized views pre-calculate and store the results of complex queries, offering significant performance gains for frequently accessed data. Selecting the right combination of these techniques depends on the specific characteristics of your data and query patterns. Regular monitoring and analysis of query performance are essential to identify bottlenecks and optimize accordingly.

Data visualization transforms raw data into easily digestible visual representations. Charts, graphs, and dashboards allow users to quickly grasp trends, patterns, and outliers within the data. Effective data visualization requires choosing the appropriate chart type for the data being presented. For instance, line charts are ideal for showing trends over time, while bar charts are better suited for comparing values across different categories. Furthermore, adhering to visualization best practices, such as using clear labels, appropriate color schemes, and minimizing clutter, is crucial for creating effective and insightful visualizations. Several tools and libraries are available to facilitate data visualization, ranging from simple spreadsheet software to sophisticated business intelligence platforms. Selecting the right tool depends on the complexity of your visualization needs and your budget.

Reporting and Business Intelligence (BI) tools empower users to create interactive dashboards and reports that provide actionable insights. These tools offer a range of features, including data connectivity, data manipulation, visualization, and reporting. Choosing the right BI tool depends on factors such as the size and complexity of your data warehouse, the technical expertise of your users, and your budget. Some popular BI platforms include Tableau, Power BI, and Qlik Sense. These tools offer a variety of functionalities, from creating interactive dashboards to generating pixel-perfect reports. Learning to effectively use these tools allows you to translate data into actionable intelligence, empowering business users to make informed decisions. By mastering the techniques discussed in this chapter, you can unlock the full potential of your data warehouse, transforming raw data into a valuable asset for your organization.

5.1 SQL for Data Warehousing

A well-structured data warehouse empowers analysts with the ability to derive meaningful insights swiftly. Structured Query Language (SQL) plays a pivotal role in this process, providing the primary means of interacting with the data. While standard SQL knowledge is a prerequisite, data warehousing often demands specialized queries to leverage the dimensional model effectively. This chapter will equip you with the essential SQL skills for navigating and analyzing data within a data warehouse environment. Understanding the nuances of the dimensional model, particularly the relationship between fact and dimension tables, is crucial. Your queries will frequently involve joins between these tables, allowing you to analyze data within specific contexts.

Consider a scenario where you need to analyze sales data. Your fact table might contain information on sales transactions, including product ID, customer ID, date, and sales amount. The associated dimension tables would provide detailed information about the products (product name, category, price), customers (name, location, demographics), and time (date, month, year). To understand sales performance by product category, you would use a SQL query joining the sales fact table with the product dimension table. This join operation allows you to associate each sales transaction with the corresponding product category, enabling aggregated analysis.

Aggregation functions are your primary tools for summarizing data within a data warehouse. SUM, AVG, COUNT, MIN, and MAX are frequently used to calculate totals, averages, counts, minimums, and maximums, respectively. For instance, calculating total sales by month would involve summing the sales amount from the fact table, grouping the results by the month attribute from the time dimension table. These functions empower analysts to derive insights from large datasets, summarizing data into meaningful metrics.

Filtering and grouping are essential for focusing on specific data subsets. WHERE clauses filter records based on specific criteria, while GROUP BY clauses group records with the same values in specified columns. Suppose you need to analyze sales for a specific product category in a particular region. Your query would include a WHERE clause to filter sales records based on the product category and customer region, joined with their respective dimension tables. Subsequently, a GROUP BY clause can be used to aggregate sales data by customer demographics within that filtered subset.

Window functions provide a powerful way to perform calculations across a set of rows related to the current row, without grouping the results. These functions are especially useful for calculating running totals, moving averages, and rankings. For example, calculating the cumulative sales for each product over time would involve using a window function to sum sales for each product up to the current date. This allows for trend analysis without losing the granularity of individual sales transactions.

Common Table Expressions (CTEs) improve query readability and maintainability, especially for complex queries. CTEs are temporary, named result sets defined within a single query. They can be referenced multiple times within the same query, simplifying the logic and making it easier to understand. For example, if you need to calculate the percentage of total sales contributed by each product category, you could use a CTE to calculate total sales first, then reference this CTE in a subsequent query to calculate the percentage contribution of each category. This modular approach enhances code clarity and reduces redundancy.

Stored procedures encapsulate a set of SQL statements that can be reused across multiple queries and applications. They improve performance by reducing network traffic and allowing the database server to optimize execution plans. Creating stored procedures for frequently used queries, like calculating daily sales reports or customer segmentation analysis, simplifies data access for other users and applications. These procedures ensure consistency in data retrieval and analysis across the organization.

Data warehousing involves working with large datasets, so optimizing query performance is paramount. Understanding how indexes work and using them appropriately can significantly improve query speed. Creating indexes on frequently queried columns, particularly those involved in joins and filters, allows the database to quickly locate the required data without scanning the entire table. Analyzing query execution plans can help identify performance bottlenecks and guide indexing strategies.

Furthermore, understanding the underlying data model and choosing appropriate join types can significantly impact performance. Inner joins retrieve only matching records from both tables, while outer joins retrieve all records from one table and matching records from the other. Choosing the right join type depends on the specific requirements of the query and the desired results.

Finally, partitioning large tables can dramatically improve query performance. Partitioning divides a table into smaller, more manageable segments based on a specific column, typically a date or category. When a query filters data based on the partitioning column, the database only needs to access the relevant partitions, reducing the amount of data scanned and improving query speed.

5.2 OLAP and MDX

Online Analytical Processing (OLAP) empowers users to analyze data from multiple perspectives, uncovering hidden trends and patterns. Unlike traditional relational databases optimized for transactional processing, OLAP systems are designed for complex analytical queries across large datasets. Imagine navigating a multidimensional cube where each dimension represents a different attribute, like time, product, or location. OLAP enables you to slice and dice this cube, drilling down into specific details or rolling up to broader summaries. This multidimensional approach offers a powerful way to understand the interplay of various factors influencing your business.

Multidimensional Expressions (MDX) is the query language specifically designed for OLAP. Think of it as a specialized tool for navigating that multidimensional cube. While SQL excels at retrieving individual records, MDX retrieves aggregated data based on dimensions and hierarchies. For instance, you could use MDX to calculate the total sales for a specific product category in a particular region over a given time period. This ability to perform complex calculations across multiple dimensions is what makes MDX invaluable for analytical reporting. Learning MDX involves understanding its core components: axes, members, sets, tuples, and functions.

Axes define the perspective of your query. Picture them as the edges of your multidimensional cube. Typically, MDX queries have at least two axes: rows and columns. These axes hold the members you want to analyze. Members are the specific values within each dimension. For example, "January 2024" would be a member of the "Time" dimension. Sets are collections of members, allowing you to analyze multiple values simultaneously. A set could include all months in a quarter or all products in a specific category. Tuples combine members from different dimensions, creating coordinates within your cube. A tuple might represent the sales of a particular product in a specific region during a given month.

MDX functions enable a wide range of calculations and manipulations. These functions can aggregate data, calculate ratios, perform time-based analysis, and much more. Mastering MDX functions is crucial for extracting meaningful insights from your data. Understanding how these components interact is key to writing effective MDX queries. By combining axes, members, sets, tuples, and functions, you can precisely target the information you need and retrieve the answers you seek.

Moving from theoretical concepts to practical implementation requires a clear understanding of how MDX queries are structured. A typical MDX query begins with the SELECT keyword, followed by the data you want to retrieve. This is specified using MDX expressions that define the axes and calculations. The FROM clause indicates the cube you are querying. The WHERE clause filters the data based on specific criteria, similar to SQL. Let's delve into a practical example to illustrate how MDX works in a real-world scenario. Consider a sales cube with dimensions for Time, Product, and Region.

Suppose you want to analyze the sales performance of different product categories in the North and South regions over the last quarter. Your MDX query would start by selecting the measures you want to analyze, such as "Sales Amount". You would then define the rows axis using the members of the Product dimension, specifically the different product categories. The columns axis would contain the members of the Region dimension, namely "North" and "South". Finally, you would filter the data in the WHERE clause to include only the last quarter in the Time dimension. This query would return a result set showing the sales amount for each product category in the North and South regions for the specified time period. This information can then be used to identify trends, compare performance, and make informed business decisions.

The true power of MDX lies in its ability to handle complex analytical queries that are difficult, if not impossible, to achieve with standard SQL. For instance, you can calculate year-over-year growth, perform trend analysis, and calculate running totals – all within a single MDX query. These capabilities make MDX an indispensable tool for data analysts and business intelligence professionals. As you delve deeper into MDX, you'll discover a rich set of functions and features that enable even more sophisticated analysis.

Another essential aspect of working with MDX is understanding how to effectively leverage hierarchies within your dimensions. Hierarchies provide a structured way to navigate and aggregate data at different levels of granularity. For example, a Time dimension might have a hierarchy that rolls up from days to months to quarters to years. This allows you to easily analyze data at the desired level of detail. By utilizing hierarchies in your MDX queries, you can perform drill-down and roll-up operations, gaining deeper insights into your data. This hierarchical navigation is a key feature of OLAP and MDX, enabling dynamic exploration of multidimensional data. Mastering this aspect of MDX will significantly enhance your ability to perform complex analytical queries.

Finally, remember that optimizing MDX queries for performance is crucial when dealing with large datasets. Techniques such as pre-aggregating data, using appropriate indexes, and optimizing the query structure can significantly improve query execution time. As you gain more experience with MDX, you'll develop a deeper understanding of these optimization strategies.

5.3 Performance Tuning

Efficient data retrieval is the lifeblood of a successful data warehouse. A well-designed warehouse can house petabytes of information, but if accessing that data is slow or cumbersome, its value diminishes significantly. This chapter dives into the critical techniques of performance tuning, enabling you to optimize query execution and unlock the true potential of your data warehouse. We'll explore indexing strategies, query optimization, and efficient data partitioning methods. By mastering these techniques, you can ensure that your data warehouse delivers timely insights to drive informed decision-making.

One of the most fundamental performance tuning techniques is indexing. Indexes are specialized data structures that allow the database to quickly locate specific rows without scanning the entire table. Think of them as the index of a book: instead of flipping through every page to find a specific topic, you can consult the index for a direct pointer. In data warehousing, several types of indexes exist, each suited to particular query patterns. Bitmap indexes are particularly efficient for low-cardinality columns, where the number of distinct values is relatively small. B-tree indexes, on the other hand, excel at handling high-cardinality columns with a wider range of values. Choosing the right index type is crucial for optimal query performance.

Beyond indexing, optimizing the queries themselves is paramount. A poorly written query can bring even the most powerful data warehouse to its knees. Analyze your queries carefully, looking for areas where you can improve efficiency. One common pitfall is using wildcard characters at the beginning of a search pattern. This forces the database to scan every row in the table, negating the benefits of indexing. Instead, try to be as specific as possible in your WHERE clauses, providing the database with as much information as possible to narrow down the search space. Additionally, avoid using functions within WHERE clauses, as this can prevent the database from utilizing indexes effectively.

Partitioning your data can significantly improve query performance, particularly for large tables. By dividing a table into smaller, more manageable chunks, you reduce the amount of data the database needs to scan for each query. Several partitioning strategies exist, each with its own advantages and disadvantages. Range partitioning divides the data based on a continuous range of values, such as dates or numerical identifiers. List partitioning, on the other hand, assigns rows to partitions based on a predefined list of values. Hash partitioning distributes rows across partitions using a hash function, providing a more even distribution of data. Choosing the appropriate partitioning strategy depends on the characteristics of your data and the types of queries you typically execute.

Materialized views offer another powerful tool for optimizing query performance. These pre-computed result sets are stored as physical tables, effectively caching the results of complex queries. When a query matching the materialized view's definition is executed, the database can retrieve the results directly from the materialized view, bypassing the need to re-execute the original query. This can dramatically improve response times, especially for frequently accessed or computationally intensive queries. However, maintaining materialized views adds overhead, as they must be refreshed whenever the underlying data changes. Carefully consider the trade-off between performance gains and maintenance costs when deciding whether to implement materialized views.

Analyzing query execution plans provides invaluable insights into how the database processes your queries. These plans detail the steps the database takes to retrieve the requested data, including the indexes used, the join algorithms employed, and the order of operations. By examining the execution plan, you can identify bottlenecks and areas for optimization. For instance, a full table scan indicates that an index is not being used effectively. A nested loop join might be less efficient than a hash join for large tables. Understanding query execution plans allows you to fine-tune your queries and indexing strategies for optimal performance.

Statistics play a vital role in query optimization. The database relies on statistics about the data, such as the distribution of values and the frequency of different data patterns, to make informed decisions about how to execute queries. Keeping these statistics up-to-date is essential for ensuring optimal performance. Outdated statistics can lead to inefficient query plans, resulting in slower response times. Regularly updating statistics, especially after significant data changes, allows the database to make better-informed decisions about query execution. Many database systems provide automated tools for gathering and updating statistics.

Furthermore, understand the nuances of your specific database system. Different database platforms have their own unique optimizations and performance tuning features. Familiarize yourself with the specific capabilities of your chosen database and leverage its strengths to maximize performance. Explore advanced features such as query hints, which provide the database with specific instructions on how to execute a query, and parallel query execution, which allows the database to distribute the workload across multiple processors for faster processing. By mastering the intricacies of your database system, you can unlock its full potential and achieve optimal performance.

Continuous monitoring and tuning are crucial for maintaining a high-performing data warehouse. Regularly review query performance, analyze execution plans, and adjust indexing and partitioning strategies as needed to adapt to changing data volumes and query patterns.

5.4 Data Visualization Techniques

Effective data visualization transforms raw data into compelling narratives, revealing hidden patterns and facilitating informed decision-making. Within the context of a data warehouse, visualization acts as a bridge between complex datasets and actionable insights. Choosing the right visualization technique depends heavily on the type of data being analyzed and the specific questions you're trying to answer. Understanding these techniques empowers you to unlock the full potential of your data warehouse and communicate its value effectively.

One common approach is the use of charts and graphs. Bar charts, for instance, excel at comparing values across different categories. They allow viewers to quickly grasp the relative magnitude of data points, making them ideal for showcasing sales figures by region or product category. Line charts, conversely, are better suited for visualizing trends over time. They can effectively illustrate stock market fluctuations, website traffic patterns, or changes in customer demographics over a given period. Scatter plots, yet another valuable tool, reveal correlations between two variables. Imagine plotting customer satisfaction against purchase frequency; a scatter plot could uncover a potential link between these metrics, informing targeted marketing strategies.

Beyond basic charts, more specialized visualizations offer deeper insights. Heatmaps represent data values as colors on a two-dimensional grid. This technique is particularly powerful for visualizing large datasets and identifying clusters or outliers. Consider a website analytics heatmap showing user engagement across different pages. Hotter colors indicate high activity, immediately highlighting popular content and potentially revealing areas for improvement. Treemaps display hierarchical data as nested rectangles, with the size of each rectangle representing the relative value of the data point. This approach can be used to visualize the market share of different companies within an industry, allowing for quick comparison of relative sizes and identification of dominant players. Network diagrams visualize relationships between entities, represented as nodes connected by edges. They can be useful for analyzing social networks, supply chains, or even the interconnectedness of departments within an organization.

Choosing the right visualization tool is equally crucial. Modern Business Intelligence (BI) platforms offer a wealth of options, ranging from interactive dashboards to customizable reports. Tableau, for example, is known for its drag-and-drop interface and ability to create visually stunning dashboards. Power BI, another popular choice, seamlessly integrates with Microsoft Excel and other Office products, making it a convenient option for many organizations. Qlik Sense and Looker are other robust BI tools that provide advanced visualization capabilities and data exploration features. Selecting a tool that aligns with your organization's needs and technical capabilities is paramount. Consider the specific audience when crafting visualizations. A presentation to the C-suite requires concise, high-level dashboards focusing on key performance indicators (KPIs). Conversely, a report for data analysts might involve more granular visualizations, allowing for deeper exploration of the data. Always aim for clarity and conciseness. Avoid cluttering visualizations with unnecessary details, and ensure labels and titles are clear and informative. A well-designed visualization should tell a story, guiding the viewer towards meaningful insights without overwhelming them with information.

Interactive visualizations add another layer of engagement, allowing users to explore data dynamically. Filtering, drilling down, and highlighting specific data points empower users to uncover insights relevant to their individual needs. Imagine a sales dashboard where users can filter by region, product, or time period. This interactivity fosters a deeper understanding of the data and promotes data-driven decision-making at all levels of the organization.

Remember, data visualization is not simply about creating aesthetically pleasing charts. It's about transforming data into actionable insights that drive business value. By carefully selecting the appropriate techniques, tools, and design principles, you can unlock the full potential of your data warehouse and empower your organization to make informed decisions based on data-driven evidence. Continuously refining your visualization strategies, experimenting with new techniques, and staying updated on the latest tools will ensure that your data warehouse remains a valuable asset in the ongoing pursuit of business success. Effective communication of these insights, whether through interactive dashboards or compelling presentations, is the final step in realizing the full value of your data warehousing efforts. Through a well-crafted visualization, a complex dataset can be transformed into a powerful narrative, driving informed decisions and contributing to organizational success.

5.5 Reporting and BI Tools

Unlocking the power of your data warehouse involves more than just storing and organizing information. It requires the ability to extract meaningful insights, visualize trends, and communicate findings effectively. This is where reporting and Business Intelligence (BI) tools come into play. They bridge the gap between raw data and actionable knowledge, empowering businesses to make data-driven decisions. Choosing the right tools is crucial, as the effectiveness of your analysis hinges on their capabilities. This chapter will explore the landscape of reporting and BI tools, helping you navigate the diverse options and select the best fit for your needs. We'll cover key features to consider, different types of tools available, and practical guidance for integrating them with your data warehouse.

From simple data summaries to complex statistical modeling, reporting and BI tools offer a wide spectrum of functionalities. Basic reporting tools excel at generating formatted reports, often with customizable templates and dashboards. These reports can present key performance indicators (KPIs), sales figures, customer demographics, and other relevant metrics in an easily digestible format. More advanced BI tools incorporate interactive visualizations, data mining algorithms, predictive modeling, and what-if analysis. These capabilities allow users to not only understand current trends but also forecast future outcomes and explore different scenarios. Consider a retail company analyzing sales data. A basic report might show total sales by region. A BI tool, however, could uncover seasonal buying patterns, identify underperforming product lines, and predict the impact of a promotional campaign.

When evaluating reporting and BI tools, consider factors like data connectivity, visualization options, ease of use, and scalability. Seamless integration with your data warehouse is paramount, ensuring efficient data transfer and minimizing manual intervention. Look for tools that support various data sources, including relational databases, cloud platforms, and flat files. Robust visualization capabilities are essential for transforming raw data into compelling visuals. Charts, graphs, maps, and dashboards should be customizable and interactive, enabling users to explore data from different angles. User-friendliness is another critical factor, especially for non-technical users. Intuitive interfaces, drag-and-drop functionalities, and pre-built templates can simplify the reporting process and empower business users to create their own reports. Finally, consider scalability to accommodate growing data volumes and evolving business needs. The chosen tool should be able to handle increasing data loads and user concurrency without compromising performance.

The market offers a plethora of reporting and BI tools, each with its own strengths and weaknesses. Traditional on-premises solutions often provide extensive customization options and control over data security. However, they typically require significant upfront investment and ongoing maintenance. Cloud-based BI platforms, on the other hand, offer greater flexibility and scalability with subscription-based pricing models. They typically require less IT infrastructure and offer easier deployment. Open-source BI tools provide a cost-effective alternative, especially for smaller organizations or those with specialized needs. However, they may require more technical expertise to implement and maintain. The best choice depends on your specific requirements, budget, and technical capabilities.

Integrating reporting and BI tools with your data warehouse requires careful planning and execution. Start by defining your reporting requirements and identifying the key metrics you need to track. Then, select the appropriate tools based on your needs and budget. Establish a secure and efficient data pipeline to connect the tools to your data warehouse. This may involve using ETL processes, API integrations, or dedicated connectors. Once the integration is complete, thoroughly test the system to ensure data accuracy and performance. Finally, provide training to your users to maximize the value of your investment in reporting and BI tools. By empowering users to access and analyze data effectively, you can unlock the full potential of your data warehouse and drive better business outcomes.

Consider the example of a healthcare organization analyzing patient data. They might use a BI tool to identify patients at high risk of readmission. By analyzing factors like age, diagnosis, and previous hospital stays, the tool can generate a predictive model. This information can then be used to implement proactive interventions, such as follow-up appointments and personalized care plans, to reduce readmission rates. This not only improves patient outcomes but also optimizes resource allocation. Another example is a manufacturing company using reporting tools to monitor production efficiency. By tracking metrics like production time, defect rates, and machine downtime, they can identify bottlenecks and areas for improvement. This data-driven approach can lead to increased productivity, reduced costs, and enhanced product quality. These real-world examples demonstrate the tangible benefits of effectively leveraging reporting and BI tools in conjunction with a well-designed data warehouse. They empower organizations to transform raw data into actionable insights, leading to informed decisions and improved business performance.

6 Chapter 6: Building a Data Warehouse

Embarking on a data warehouse project is a significant undertaking. Success hinges on meticulous planning and a clear understanding of the business requirements. This phase should involve stakeholders from various departments, including business analysts, data architects, and IT professionals. Begin by defining the scope of the data warehouse. What specific business questions are you trying to answer? Which data sources are essential? Establishing these parameters early helps prevent scope creep and ensures the project remains focused on delivering value. Next, gather detailed requirements regarding data sources, data quality expectations, reporting needs, and performance requirements. This information forms the foundation for the design and implementation phases. A comprehensive requirements document should be created, reviewed, and approved by all stakeholders. This document serves as a blueprint throughout the project lifecycle.

Once the requirements are solidified, the design phase can begin. This stage translates the business requirements into a technical blueprint for the data warehouse. A crucial aspect is choosing the appropriate architecture. Will you opt for a traditional Kimball-style dimensional model, a data vault, or a hybrid approach? The choice depends on factors like the complexity of your data, the reporting requirements, and the skills of your team. Data modeling is another critical component. Design your fact and dimension tables carefully, ensuring they accurately reflect the business processes and enable efficient querying. Consider data types, keys, and relationships between tables. Performance considerations should also be factored in, such as indexing strategies and partitioning schemes. A well-designed schema ensures efficient data storage and retrieval. Documenting the design decisions, including data lineage and transformation rules, is essential for future maintenance and modifications.

The implementation phase brings the design to life. This involves building the ETL pipelines to extract data from source systems, transform it according to the defined rules, and load it into the data warehouse. Choosing the right ETL tool is crucial for efficiency. Consider factors like data volume, complexity of transformations, and integration with your existing infrastructure. Thorough testing is paramount throughout the implementation process. Unit testing validates individual components, while integration testing ensures the entire ETL process works seamlessly. System testing checks the overall performance and functionality of the data warehouse. Establish a robust testing framework and create test cases that cover all scenarios.

Deployment marks the transition from development to production. There are various deployment strategies, each with its advantages and disadvantages. A full deployment involves replacing the existing system with the new data warehouse at once. This approach is straightforward but carries a higher risk. A phased deployment rolls out the data warehouse incrementally, minimizing disruption but potentially extending the overall project timeline. A parallel deployment runs both the old and new systems concurrently, allowing for thorough comparison and validation. Choose the strategy that best suits your organization's risk tolerance and operational needs. After deployment, ongoing monitoring and maintenance are crucial. Regularly monitor system performance, data quality, and user feedback. Implement a process for handling incidents and resolving issues promptly. Establish a clear communication channel for users to report problems and request enhancements.

Finally, documentation plays a vital role throughout the entire process. Comprehensive documentation ensures maintainability, facilitates troubleshooting, and supports future enhancements. Document everything from the initial requirements to the technical design, ETL processes, and deployment procedures. Use clear and concise language, diagrams, and examples to make the documentation easy to understand and use. Maintain a version control system for all documentation to track changes and ensure consistency. Treat your documentation as a living document, updating it as the data warehouse evolves. Remember, a well-documented data warehouse is easier to manage, adapt, and expand as your business needs change. This careful approach to each phase will contribute significantly to a successful and valuable data warehousing initiative.

6.1 Planning and Requirements

A successful data warehouse implementation hinges on meticulous planning and a thorough understanding of business requirements. This phase sets the stage for the entire project, influencing design choices, resource allocation, and ultimately, the delivered solution's efficacy. It involves a systematic approach to define the scope, identify data sources, establish key performance indicators (KPIs), and outline the project's timeline and budget. Think of this stage as the blueprint for your data warehouse – a roadmap that guides every subsequent decision. Skipping this crucial step often leads to costly rework, delays, and a final product that fails to meet business needs.

Begin by defining the scope. Clearly articulate the business problems the data warehouse aims to address. What specific questions should it answer? Which departments will use it, and for what purposes? For example, a sales team might need insights into product performance, while marketing may require customer segmentation data. Precisely defining the scope ensures that the data warehouse remains focused on delivering relevant information and avoids becoming an unwieldy repository of unused data. This focus also helps to manage expectations and maintain stakeholder alignment throughout the project.

Identifying and understanding relevant data sources is crucial. Data warehouses often integrate information from disparate systems – CRM, ERP, marketing automation platforms, and more. Catalog each source, noting its data structure, accessibility, and data quality. Understanding the nuances of each source, such as data formats, update frequencies, and potential data quality issues, is essential for designing effective extraction processes. This detailed inventory also aids in estimating the effort required for data integration and cleansing.

Next, establish key performance indicators (KPIs). These metrics will measure the data warehouse's success in meeting business objectives. KPIs should be specific, measurable, achievable, relevant, and time-bound (SMART). For instance, a KPI could be to reduce the time required to generate sales reports by 50% or to improve customer retention rates by 10%. Defining KPIs early on ensures that the data warehouse is designed to deliver the information needed to track and analyze these critical metrics.

Develop a realistic timeline and budget. Building a data warehouse is a complex undertaking, requiring significant resources, both human and financial. The timeline should account for each stage of the project, from requirements gathering and design to implementation, testing, and deployment. Similarly, the budget should encompass hardware, software, personnel, training, and ongoing maintenance costs. A well-defined timeline and budget allows for effective resource allocation and helps to avoid cost overruns and delays. Be prepared to justify the budget to stakeholders, highlighting the long-term return on investment that the data warehouse can deliver.

User acceptance testing is an integral part of the planning process. Engage end-users early and often to ensure the data warehouse meets their specific needs. Conduct regular feedback sessions throughout the development process. These sessions provide invaluable insights into data requirements, reporting needs, and usability considerations. User involvement ensures that the final product is intuitive, user-friendly, and delivers the information they need in a readily accessible format. This proactive approach minimizes the risk of developing a system that fails to meet user expectations.

Documenting the entire planning process is vital. Create a comprehensive requirements document that details the project scope, data sources, KPIs, timeline, budget, and user feedback. This document serves as a single source of truth throughout the project lifecycle, ensuring that everyone involved is aligned on the project goals and objectives. This documentation also provides a valuable resource for future maintenance and enhancements. It allows for easier troubleshooting, knowledge transfer, and adaptation to evolving business needs.

Consider future scalability and flexibility. Business requirements and data volumes are likely to change over time. Design the data warehouse with scalability in mind, ensuring it can accommodate future growth and evolving data needs. This forward-thinking approach minimizes the need for costly and time-consuming system overhauls down the line. Flexibility in design also allows the data warehouse to adapt to new data sources and analytical requirements.

Finally, remember that data governance is essential. Establish clear policies and procedures for data quality, access control, and security. Data governance ensures the reliability, integrity, and confidentiality of the data within the warehouse. It also helps to comply with relevant regulations and industry best practices. A robust data governance framework builds trust in the data and fosters informed decision-making. This framework should be clearly defined and communicated to all stakeholders involved in the data warehouse project.

6.2 Implementation and Deployment

Translating the blueprint of your data warehouse design into a functioning system requires careful consideration of several implementation and deployment aspects. This stage marks the culmination of your meticulous planning and design efforts, bringing your vision for insightful data analysis to life. A systematic approach to implementation ensures a smooth transition from design to a fully operational data warehouse.

Begin by prioritizing the development and deployment of core components. Focus on the most critical data sources and business processes initially. This iterative approach allows for early validation of the design and provides valuable feedback for subsequent iterations. It also minimizes the risk associated with large-scale deployments by allowing you to identify and address potential issues in a controlled environment. Think of it as building a strong foundation before adding the intricate details.

Data migration is a crucial step that demands careful planning and execution. Before transferring data, thoroughly cleanse and validate it to maintain data quality and integrity within the warehouse. Establish a robust process for data extraction, transformation, and loading (ETL) to ensure consistent and reliable data delivery. Consider using automated ETL tools to streamline this process and minimize manual intervention. Thorough testing of the ETL process is paramount to identify and rectify any data inconsistencies before they impact the warehouse.

Implementing robust monitoring and logging mechanisms is essential for ongoing maintenance and troubleshooting. Real-time monitoring of key performance indicators (KPIs) like data load times, query performance, and storage utilization helps ensure the health and efficiency of your data warehouse. Detailed logging provides invaluable insights into system behavior, enabling you to proactively identify and address potential issues. This proactive approach minimizes downtime and ensures the continuous availability of your data warehouse.

User acceptance testing (UAT) is a critical validation step before full deployment. Involving end-users in this process ensures the data warehouse meets their specific requirements and provides the intended value. Their feedback helps identify any usability issues or discrepancies between the design and the actual implementation. This collaborative approach ensures the data warehouse is a valuable tool for the intended audience.

Deploying the data warehouse involves a strategic rollout plan. Consider a phased approach, starting with a pilot group of users and gradually expanding access to the wider organization. This allows for controlled management of user onboarding and system load, minimizing disruption to existing operations. Continuous monitoring and performance tuning during this phase ensure the system remains stable and responsive as the user base grows.

Post-implementation, ongoing maintenance and optimization are crucial for long-term success. Regularly review system performance and identify areas for improvement. Implement performance tuning strategies to optimize query execution and data retrieval. Stay abreast of evolving business needs and adapt the data warehouse accordingly. This proactive approach ensures the data warehouse remains a valuable asset for years to come.

Documentation throughout the implementation and deployment process is essential.

Maintaining comprehensive documentation of system architecture, data models, ETL processes, and operational procedures provides a valuable resource for ongoing maintenance and troubleshooting. Clear and concise documentation facilitates knowledge transfer and ensures continuity in the event of staff changes. It also serves as a valuable reference for future enhancements and expansions of the data warehouse.

Training users on how to effectively utilize the data warehouse is a crucial investment. Provide comprehensive training programs that cover data access, querying, and reporting. Empower users to generate meaningful insights from the data and translate them into actionable business decisions. Well-trained users can maximize the value of the data warehouse, contributing to a higher return on investment.

Security considerations are paramount throughout the entire lifecycle of the data warehouse. Implement robust security measures to protect sensitive data from unauthorized access. This includes access control mechanisms, data encryption, and regular security audits. Staying informed about evolving security threats and implementing necessary safeguards ensures the confidentiality and integrity of your data.

Finally, remember that building a data warehouse is an ongoing journey, not a destination. Business requirements and data landscapes are constantly evolving. Embrace a flexible and adaptable approach to data warehousing, allowing for continuous improvement and expansion. By staying proactive and responsive to changing needs, your data warehouse can remain a valuable asset, driving informed decision-making and contributing to the success of your organization. The ability to adapt and evolve is key to maximizing the long-term value of your data warehouse investment.

7 Chapter 7: Advanced Data Warehousing

The data warehousing landscape is constantly evolving. Traditional on-premises solutions are increasingly giving way to cloud-based alternatives, offering scalability, flexibility, and cost-effectiveness. Cloud-based data warehousing leverages the power of cloud computing to provide on-demand resources, eliminating the need for extensive hardware investments and maintenance. Providers like Snowflake, Amazon Redshift, and Google BigQuery offer fully managed services, handling infrastructure, security, and software updates, allowing organizations to focus on data analysis rather than infrastructure management. These platforms offer features like auto-scaling, which dynamically adjusts computing resources based on workload demands, ensuring optimal performance during peak periods without overspending on idle capacity. Furthermore, cloud data warehouses facilitate seamless integration with other cloud services, creating a unified data ecosystem for comprehensive analytics.

One key advantage of cloud data warehousing is its elasticity. Businesses can quickly scale their storage and computing resources up or down depending on their evolving needs. This is particularly beneficial for organizations experiencing fluctuating data volumes or seasonal peaks in demand. Imagine a retail company during the holiday season: they can effortlessly scale up their cloud data warehouse to handle the surge in transactional data, then scale back down once the peak subsides, paying only for the resources consumed. This dynamic scalability allows for agile responses to changing business requirements and optimizes cost efficiency. Moreover, cloud platforms often provide pay-as-you-go pricing models, further enhancing cost control.

The concept of a data lake has emerged as a complementary approach to traditional data warehousing. A data lake is a vast repository of raw, unstructured data in its native format. Unlike the structured, schema-on-read approach of data warehouses, data lakes store data in its original form, allowing for flexible exploration and analysis of diverse data types. Integrating a data lake with a data warehouse can provide a powerful combination for comprehensive insights. The data lake can serve as a landing zone for all incoming data, while the data warehouse houses the refined, structured data used for specific business intelligence applications. This integration allows organizations to leverage the agility of a data lake for data exploration and discovery, while maintaining the performance and structure of a data warehouse for reporting and analysis. It creates a holistic data environment, bridging the gap between raw data and actionable insights. Implementing this integration requires careful planning and execution. Data governance and metadata management are crucial to ensure data quality and discoverability within the combined environment. Tools and processes must be established to efficiently move data from the data lake to the data warehouse after appropriate cleansing and transformation. This might involve using specialized ETL tools or leveraging cloud-based data integration services. Consider the scenario of a healthcare organization collecting patient data from various sources: the data lake can store all raw data, including medical images and doctor's notes, while the data warehouse houses structured patient demographics and clinical data for reporting and analysis. This integrated approach allows for both detailed exploration of raw data and efficient querying of structured information.

Real-time data warehousing is another significant advancement. Traditional data warehouses often operate on a batch processing schedule, updating data at regular intervals, typically daily or weekly. However, in today's fast-paced business environment, the demand for immediate insights is growing rapidly. Real-time data warehousing allows organizations to capture, process, and analyze data as it's generated, providing up-to-the-minute visibility into key business metrics. This enables proactive decision-making and faster responses to changing market conditions. Imagine a financial institution monitoring stock prices: a real-time data warehouse can provide immediate alerts on significant price fluctuations, enabling traders to react swiftly and capitalize on market opportunities. This immediacy can be the difference between success and failure in time-sensitive situations.

Implementing a real-time data warehouse requires a different architectural approach than traditional batch-oriented systems. Data ingestion must be continuous, using technologies like change data capture or streaming data platforms. The data processing pipeline must be optimized for low latency, ensuring that data is processed and made available for analysis with minimal delay. This often involves using in-memory databases or specialized stream processing engines. Consider an e-commerce website tracking customer behavior: real-time data warehousing allows them to analyze clickstream data and immediately personalize product recommendations or offer targeted promotions, enhancing customer experience and driving sales. This real-time responsiveness is crucial for staying competitive in the digital age. Therefore, integrating these advanced techniques into a data warehousing strategy empowers organizations with comprehensive, timely insights, driving data-driven decision making and enhancing business agility.

7.1 Cloud-Based Warehousing

The cloud has fundamentally reshaped the data warehousing landscape. Gone are the days of massive upfront investments in hardware and software licenses. Cloud-based warehousing offers scalability, flexibility, and cost-effectiveness previously unattainable for many organizations. This shift allows businesses of all sizes to leverage the power of advanced analytics and gain valuable insights from their data. Consider the implications for a rapidly growing startup: instead of procuring and managing physical servers, they can simply provision warehouse resources on demand, scaling up or down as needed. This agility translates directly into competitive advantage.

Cloud-based data warehouses provide a compelling alternative to traditional on-premise solutions. They offer several key advantages, including reduced infrastructure costs. By eliminating the need for physical hardware, organizations can significantly lower their capital expenditures. Maintenance and administration are also streamlined; cloud providers handle the underlying infrastructure, freeing up internal IT teams to focus on higher-value tasks like data analysis and business intelligence. Consider the case of a retail company analyzing customer purchase patterns: a cloud-based warehouse allows them to quickly process large datasets and identify trends without managing complex hardware configurations.

There are several prominent cloud-based data warehouse providers, each with its own strengths and weaknesses. Amazon Web Services (AWS) offers Redshift, a powerful and scalable solution known for its performance and integration with other AWS services. Microsoft Azure provides Synapse Analytics, a fully managed data warehouse service with robust security features and integration with the Microsoft ecosystem.

Google Cloud Platform (GCP) offers BigQuery, a serverless data warehouse known for its speed and ability to handle massive datasets. Choosing the right provider depends on specific organizational needs and existing technology investments. For example, a company heavily invested in the Microsoft ecosystem might naturally gravitate toward Azure Synapse.

Migrating an existing data warehouse to the cloud requires careful planning and execution. The first step involves assessing the current data warehouse environment and identifying any potential compatibility issues. Data migration tools and strategies can then be selected to ensure a smooth transition. Thorough testing and validation are crucial to guarantee data integrity and maintain business continuity. Imagine a financial institution migrating sensitive customer data; rigorous testing is paramount to avoid errors and maintain regulatory compliance.

Security considerations are paramount in cloud-based warehousing. Data encryption both in transit and at rest is essential to protect sensitive information from unauthorized access. Access control mechanisms, such as role-based access control (RBAC), should be implemented to restrict data access to authorized personnel only. Regular security audits and penetration testing can help identify and address vulnerabilities. Consider a healthcare organization storing patient records; stringent security measures are crucial to comply with HIPAA regulations.

Integrating a cloud-based data warehouse with existing business intelligence (BI) tools is essential for maximizing the value of data. Modern cloud warehouses offer seamless integration with a variety of BI platforms, enabling users to access and analyze data directly from their preferred tools. This integration empowers business users to create reports, dashboards, and visualizations that drive informed decision-making. Think of a marketing team analyzing campaign performance; direct integration with their BI tools allows them to quickly identify successful strategies and optimize future campaigns.

Cost optimization is a crucial aspect of managing a cloud-based data warehouse. Cloud providers offer various pricing models, and understanding these models is essential for controlling costs. Techniques like resource optimization, data lifecycle management, and reserved instance purchasing can help minimize expenses. For example, archiving infrequently accessed data to cheaper storage tiers can significantly reduce storage costs.

Future trends in cloud-based warehousing point toward increased automation and integration with other cloud services. Serverless data warehousing, which automatically scales resources based on demand, is gaining traction. Integration with machine learning and artificial intelligence platforms is also becoming more prevalent, enabling advanced analytics and predictive modeling directly within the data warehouse. Imagine a supply chain manager using machine learning to predict inventory needs based on historical data; this type of integration can streamline operations and improve efficiency.

The emergence of the data lakehouse paradigm further blurs the lines between data warehouses and data lakes. Data lakehouses combine the structured approach of a data warehouse with the flexibility of a data lake, allowing organizations to store and analyze both structured and unstructured data in a single platform. This convergence offers greater flexibility and scalability for handling diverse data types and evolving business needs. Consider a media company analyzing customer viewing habits alongside social media sentiment; a data lakehouse approach allows them to combine these disparate data sources for a more holistic view.

By understanding the nuances of cloud-based warehousing, organizations can unlock the true potential of their data. The cloud offers unprecedented scalability, flexibility, and cost-effectiveness, empowering businesses to gain actionable insights and make data-driven decisions. From startups to large enterprises, embracing cloud-based warehousing is no longer a luxury but a necessity for staying competitive in today's data-driven world.

7.2 Data Lake Integration

A data lake, with its raw, diverse data, presents a unique opportunity to enrich the analytical capabilities of a data warehouse. Integrating these two distinct but complementary components, however, requires a careful strategy. Consider the data lake as the vast reservoir of raw materials, and the data warehouse as the refined, purpose-built factory processing specific components for precise outcomes. Simply dumping the entire contents of the lake into the warehouse is inefficient and counterproductive. We need a targeted approach. This integration process hinges on understanding the business needs and selecting the relevant data subsets from the lake for refinement and loading into the warehouse.

One common approach to data lake integration involves establishing a structured pipeline. This pipeline acts as a conduit, directing the flow of information from the raw data of the lake to the structured environment of the warehouse. Within this pipeline, data undergoes several crucial transformations. Data cleansing, a critical step, involves identifying and correcting inaccuracies, inconsistencies, and missing values. Data standardization ensures uniformity by enforcing consistent formats and representations across different data sources. Data transformation molds the raw data into a structure suitable for the warehouse's dimensional model. This often involves aggregating, enriching, and filtering data according to specific business requirements.

Different data lake integration patterns exist, each suited to particular use cases. For instance, a basic approach involves directly extracting data from the lake and loading it into the warehouse after the necessary transformations. This approach works well for simpler scenarios with clearly defined data requirements. Another pattern leverages a staging area, an intermediate layer between the lake and the warehouse. This allows for more complex transformations and data quality checks before the data reaches the warehouse. A more advanced approach employs a data virtualization layer. This layer allows users to query data directly from the lake without physically moving it to the warehouse, creating a virtualized view that integrates data from both systems. Choosing the right integration pattern depends on factors like data volume, complexity, and the desired level of real-time analysis.

Security considerations are paramount when integrating a data lake with a data warehouse. Data lakes often contain sensitive information. Maintaining data security throughout the integration process is essential. Implement robust access control mechanisms to restrict data access to authorized personnel. Encryption techniques protect data both in transit and at rest. Regular security audits and monitoring help identify and mitigate potential vulnerabilities. Data governance policies provide a framework for managing data access, usage, and storage, ensuring compliance with relevant regulations and internal best practices. These security measures safeguard sensitive data and maintain the integrity of the entire data ecosystem.

Metadata management is a crucial but often overlooked aspect of data lake integration. Metadata provides valuable context about the data, including its origin, format, and meaning. Implementing a robust metadata management system enhances data discoverability, allowing analysts to easily find and understand relevant data within the lake. It also facilitates data lineage tracking, enabling users to trace the origin and transformations of data as it moves from the lake to the warehouse. This ensures data transparency and builds trust in the analytical insights derived from the integrated system. A well-managed metadata framework is essential for effective data governance and efficient use of the combined data resources.

Tools and technologies play a significant role in simplifying and automating the data lake integration process. Several cloud-based solutions offer pre-built connectors and services for seamless integration. Data integration platforms provide comprehensive tools for data ingestion, transformation, and orchestration. Cloud-based data warehouses often offer native integrations with popular data lake services, streamlining the process. Leveraging these tools significantly reduces the time and effort required for integration, allowing organizations to focus on extracting value from their data rather than managing complex infrastructure. These tools also provide features for data quality monitoring, schema evolution management, and performance optimization, ensuring a robust and efficient integration pipeline.

The integration of a data lake and a data warehouse represents a powerful synergy. The raw, diverse data of the lake complements the refined, structured data of the warehouse, offering a holistic view of the organization's information landscape. This integration, however, requires careful planning, execution, and ongoing management. By adopting a strategic approach and leveraging the appropriate tools and technologies, organizations can unlock the full potential of their data, enabling data-driven decisions and driving impactful business outcomes. Remember, the true value lies not in the individual components but in their harmonious integration. This unified data ecosystem empowers organizations with the insights needed to thrive in today's data-rich environment. The result is a comprehensive and flexible data architecture that can adapt to evolving business needs and provide valuable insights for years to come. By meticulously addressing these considerations, organizations can establish a data integration pipeline that not only functions efficiently but also lays the groundwork for future scalability and adaptability in the face of evolving data landscapes.

7.3 Real-Time Data Warehousing

The demand for immediate insights has driven the evolution of traditional data warehousing towards real-time data warehousing (RTDW). Unlike traditional warehouses that operate on batch updates, RTDW systems ingest and process data continuously, providing up-to-the-minute information for operational decision-making. This shift addresses the limitations of batch processing, where delays in data availability can hinder timely responses to changing business conditions. Consider a financial institution needing to detect fraudulent transactions as they occur. A traditional data warehouse, updating only nightly, would be inadequate. An RTDW, however, could analyze transactions in real-time, flagging suspicious activities immediately. This capability enables proactive intervention, minimizing potential losses.

Implementing an RTDW requires careful consideration of several key architectural components. Data ingestion must be streamlined to handle the constant influx of data. This often involves using change data capture (CDC) techniques, which identify and capture only the changes made to source systems rather than replicating entire datasets. This approach minimizes the volume of data needing processing, improving efficiency. Furthermore, the underlying data storage and processing infrastructure must be optimized for speed and scalability. In-memory databases, optimized for fast data retrieval and analysis, are commonly employed. Distributed processing frameworks, capable of handling massive data volumes and complex computations in parallel, also play a crucial role.

The choice of ETL process also differs significantly. Traditional ETL, designed for batch processing, is unsuitable for the continuous data flow of RTDW. Real-time ETL, often implemented using stream processing platforms like Apache Kafka or Apache Flink, takes over. These platforms allow for data transformation and enrichment as it streams into the warehouse, ensuring the data is immediately ready for analysis. Imagine a retail company tracking website traffic in real-time. Real-time ETL could enrich the clickstream data with customer demographics from a CRM system, providing immediate insights into customer behavior and preferences. This allows for real-time personalized offers and targeted marketing campaigns.

Data quality management in an RTDW presents unique challenges. Unlike batch processing where data can be validated and cleansed before loading, real-time data requires continuous monitoring and validation. Automated data quality checks and anomaly detection algorithms become critical. These systems must be capable of identifying and flagging potential data errors in real-time, preventing the propagation of inaccurate information. Consider a manufacturing company monitoring sensor data from production equipment. Real-time data quality checks could identify faulty sensor readings, preventing incorrect analysis and potentially costly production errors.

Integrating an RTDW with existing systems is another critical aspect of implementation. Often, organizations already have a traditional data warehouse in place. The RTDW should complement, not replace, this existing infrastructure. A common approach is to use the RTDW for operational reporting and real-time analytics, while the traditional data warehouse continues to handle historical reporting and more complex analytical tasks. This hybrid approach allows organizations to leverage the strengths of both systems. For example, a logistics company might use RTDW to track package locations in real-time, while using the traditional data warehouse for analyzing historical delivery performance and optimizing routes.

Finally, ensuring data consistency and accuracy across both the real-time and traditional data warehouses is essential. Data synchronization mechanisms must be in place to prevent discrepancies. This involves defining clear data governance policies and establishing data lineage tracking. This ensures that both systems reflect the same underlying truth, enabling informed decision-making at all levels. For example, a healthcare provider might use RTDW to monitor patient vital signs in real-time, while the traditional data warehouse stores comprehensive patient history. Data synchronization ensures consistency between the two systems, providing a complete and accurate view of patient health. This integrated approach empowers healthcare professionals with timely and comprehensive information for better patient care.

www.ingramcontent.com/pod-product-compliance
Lightning Source LLC
LaVergne TN
LVHW022017200926
848481LV00007B/2431
* 9 7 9 8 3 4 8 4 7 8 7 7 3 *